Short stories, plays and songs for multi-faith primary assemblies

# A World of Light

by Ruth Parmiter and Monica Price

SCHOFIELD & SIMS LTD
HUDDERSFIELD

© **1992 SCHOFIELD & SIMS LTD**

0 7217 3045 0

First printed 1992

All rights reserved. No reproduction, copy or transmission of this publication and cassette tape may be made without written permission, except under the terms set out below.

This publication and cassette tape are copyright. After purchase, teachers are free to reproduce any part of **A World of Light** provided that the copies are for use in Class or School Assemblies in the educational establishment of purchase only. For copying under any other circumstances prior permission must be obtained from the publishers and a fee may be payable. Public performances of any part of this work are not allowed.

Any person who does any unauthorised act in relation to this publication and cassette tape will be liable to criminal prosecution and civil claims for damages.

Monica Price wishes to dedicate this publication to Kitty Muggeridge and the late Malcolm Muggeridge.

Ruth Parmiter wishes to dedicate this publication to Olive Dewhurst, L.R.A.M., A.R.C.M., Singer, lecturer and music therapist.

Typesetting by Armitage Typo/Graphics Ltd, Huddersfield
Music Typesetting by Linda Lancaster
Printed in Great Britain by Page Bros, Norwich

# Contents

**UNIT 1. MULTI-FAITH**
**Song:** Song of Light: *Music*   1
          *Words*   4

**UNIT 2. CHRISTIAN**
**Play:** Casting the Net   5
**Song:** Jesus The Provider: *Music*   9
          *Words*   12

**UNIT 3. SIKH**
**Story:** The Guru and the Princes   13
**Song:** Hail, Har Gobind: *Music*   15
          *Words*   17

**UNIT 4. JEWISH**
**Play:** Moses and the Princess   18
**Play:** Moses and Aaron Beat the Magicians   24
**Song:** Moses *Music*   27
          *Words*   33

**UNIT 5. CHRISTIAN**
**Play:** The Wise and Foolish Bridesmaids   35
**Song:** Be Prepared *Music*   41
          *Words*   49

**UNIT 6. ISLAMIC**
**Story:** The Thirsty Dog   50
**Song:** The Thirsty Dog *Music*   52
          *Words*   54

**UNIT 7. BUDDHIST**
**Story:** The Lama and the Fish   55
**Play:** The Lama and the Fish   56
**Song:** The Lama and the Fish *Music*   64
          *Words*   67

**UNIT 8. JEWISH**
**Play:** Ruth and Naomi   68
**Song:** From Naomi to Ruth *Music*   78
          *Words*   82

**UNIT 9. HINDU**
**Story:** Kori's Dream   83
**Song:** Kori's Song *Music*   86
          *Words*   89

**UNIT 10. CHRISTIAN**
**Story:** A Very Special Donkey   90
**Song:** Donkey Song *Music*   93
          *Words*   98

**UNIT 11. JEWISH**
**Play:** Samuel the Boy Prophet   99
**Song:** Samuel *Music*   106
          *Words*   108

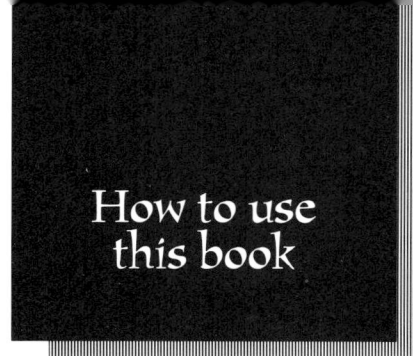

# How to use this book

## Text

This book is photocopiable, so that the teacher can present each child with his or her own copy of the complete assembly. For the short stories and plays, space has been left after the words 'Narrator' or the character name, so that the child's name can be inserted. For the plays, stage instructions are interspersed in italic type throughout the text. Each child should have a complete copy of all the assembly material so he or she knows the timing of his or her involvement in the assembly as a whole, and will not need any 'cueing' from the teacher at the time of performance.

## A World of Light

Whilst the 1988 Education Reform Act stated that the majority of acts of collective worship in any school term should be "of a broadly Christian nature", the inclusion of material from World Faiths other than Christian has also been approved. The fact that some schools may not have many pupils from non-Christian communities does not minimise the fact that both Religious Education and Collective Worship need to promote both spiritual and social awareness.

This book is intended for those Primary Schools who do include Multi-faith resources in their assembly presentations. The stories, plays and songs provide material for both the single assembly and for a thematic approach.

## Casting the Net (play)

The play presents one of Jesus' best known Resurrection appearances and suggests the disciples' (other than Peter) initial uneasy response.

Although the backdrop of a river and a darkened stage would be appropriate with the characters actually on stage in a boat, voices off stage and the use of lighting techniques to show the fishermen in silhouette will also work, though, again, this play might be presented without scenery and props but with sound effects such as water lapping to aid imagination.

## The Guru and the Princes (story)

Guru Har Gobind's imprisonment in the grim fortress created international protest in the sixteenth century. The incident forms the basis for the Sikh Divali celebration and the daring rescue of the Hindu princes might be used to illustrate such themes as caring for others and leadership. The story lends itself to dramatic presentation as well as the drawing of the Guru's actual rescue of the long neglected princes.

## Moses and the Princess (play)

The play may be presented simply with few props or more elaborately with a backdrop of the river scene. The costumes may be found in any school property cupboard, the longer dresses and head shawls of Jochabed and Miriam contrasting with the simple tunics and heavy jewellery of the Egyptian girls.

## Moses and the Magicians (play)

Shepherds' costumes from a Nativity play would be suitable for Moses and Aaron. Pharaoh and his magicians would wear long trousers or a piece of

# How to use this book

material similar to the Indian dhoti. The heads of the Egyptians would be uncovered. A sash or scarf would be worn from the left shoulder to the waist. Alternatively, the play may be presented in ordinary dress.

Pharaoh's palace might be indicated by an archway or two large pillars but a few colourful cushions would suffice and a large chair decorated in gold paper would provide a suitable throne if one is required.

A toy snake with a piece of cotton attached would suffice and be realistic enough for this scene.

## The Wise and Foolish Bridesmaids (play)

The purpose of bridesmaids nowadays contrasts sharply with the role they knew two thousand years ago when it was their duty to lead the bridegroom through the darkened streets to his wedding at whatever hour he chose to arrive.

Although the real explanation of the parable might be that Jesus is likened to the bridegroom and "being ready" may refer to being so for Jesus or for Heaven, the actual explanation will be made according to the ages of the children taking part and level of work previously done. The "Kingdom of Heaven" may refer to this life or the next but the play offers a lively and colourful presentation of Jewish wedding customs two thousand years ago.

Teachers may well enjoy a colourful presentation and almost any colour of materials may be used, though the style would, again, be similar to Nativity plays with long clothes and headresses, shawls or scarves possibly being the easiest to acquire. A darkened stage lit by the small oil lamps will be required for the play and a street backdrop could be useful for the street scenes. There should be the sounds of a party going on in the last scene.

## The Thirsty Dog (story)

Art work based on the actual incident, i.e. the desert, the camel and the dog would be appropriate, but no visual representation whatsoever should be made of the Prophet Muhammad himself, even though he told the story, as this could offend Muslims. The theme is that of kindness to animals.

## The Lama and the Fish (story/play)

The story originates from Ladakh in the Himalayan mountains where it appears that Buddhists did sometimes eat meat on certain occasions, uncommon though this may be as a general rule.

The play's main purpose is to show the disagreement of the three boys and the secret bribing of the Lama, the local leader and holy man, because none of the boys wishes to lose face before his friends. The diffusing of the situation by showing that each boy, whilst perceiving the fish's life differently is right, is shown with humour by an essentially practical Lama but the essential point is a truly Buddhist one in that each boy deprives himself of something valuable to himself. Disagreeing, fighting and making friends are common enough happenings. The Buddha's eightfold path of right action, right speech, etc., can form further useful discussion points.

A backdrop of a lake with the boys leaning over it would be useful. All the boys would wear white, dhoti-style clothes and the King's son and the Nobleman's son could be distinguished by jewellery or by garlands. The Lama would wear the traditional holy man's yellow robe. Very little scenery would be required for the Lama's room. Curtains and a chair would be enough.

# How to use this book

### Ruth and Naomi (play)

The play will provide the basis for a "friendship" theme and a simple stage set with table and chairs will be suitable for the interiors of Naomi's houses in Moab and Bethlehem. A backdrop for the field scene of reapers at work would be useful. Again the costumes worn for Christmas plays of long clothes and headresses for both men and women will be suitable.

### Kori's Dream (story)

The Hindu attitudes concerning both the rigidity of caste obligations and the use of special skills for God are suggested by this story, though its main purpose is to present God's response to prayer and how such a response might be interpreted. The story lends itself to considerable artistic presentation.

### A Very Special Donkey (story)

This story might add an extra resource during Easter week or may have value in a presentation of the employment of children in the last century. Such themes as caring, loyalty or how animals should be treated might also find the story acceptable.

### Samuel, the Boy Prophet (play)

The Temple at Shiloh can be easily presented with the use of curtains to give an air of mystery and a few wooden chairs. Samuel and Eli would lie on the floor on sleeping mats for which pieces of carpet would suffice.

Although Samuel being brought to the temple by his mother and the initial meeting as well as the night scene are well known, the situation can be used to illustrate such themes as "Listening to God" or merely "Listening".

### Music

The musical items in the book have the words and music written out in full with the words alone written out separately. This enables the teacher to distribute copies of the music appropriately, whether the child requires the lyrics only or the whole song.

The percussion parts are merely suggestion and it is left to the discretion of the music teacher to include these parts or omit them. If the teacher decides to include them, the instruments necessary will be indicated on the percussion line of the score.

### The Raga and Drone

It is perhaps a good idea for the teacher, whether he or she is playing the Raga as a left-hand accompaniment to the melody in the right hand or not, always to play the melody whilst the children are singing, to give them extra support in this different style of music.

The Ragas for Songs 6 and 9 are presented in the bass with a bass clef, because if the song is being accompanied by piano only, the Raga can take the form of an appropriate left-hand accompaniment to the melody line, being played by the right hand. The teacher will note that the Raga is a series of notes, scale-like, ascending and descending, throughout the song. It

# How to use this book

reflects the mood of the song. The Drone can be omitted, although it is an essential part of the overall make-up of Eastern song if it is added. Suggested instruments for this part could ideally be the modern-day electronic keyboard, steel drum, or the 'cello as it is a lower-stringed instrument. If these instruments are not available the teacher can play the Drone on higher sounding percussion instruments and this works sufficiently well. The important fact is that the Drone traditionally accompanies the whole song and is heard throughout.

# Song of Light

UNIT 1
A multi-faith song for assembly

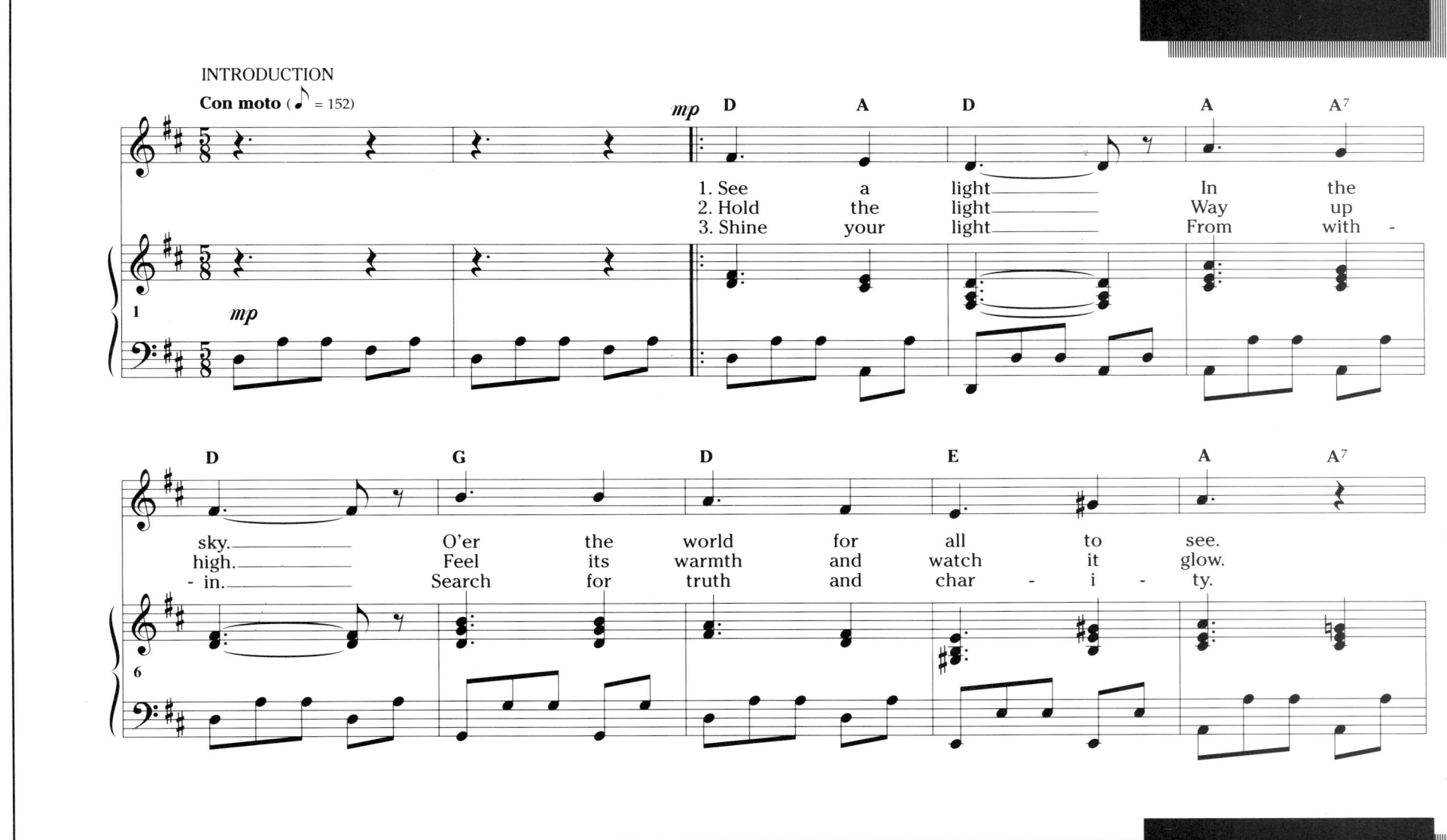

1   A WORLD OF LIGHT · SCHOFIELD & SIMS LTD

SHEET 1

# Song of Light

SHEET 2

# Song of Light

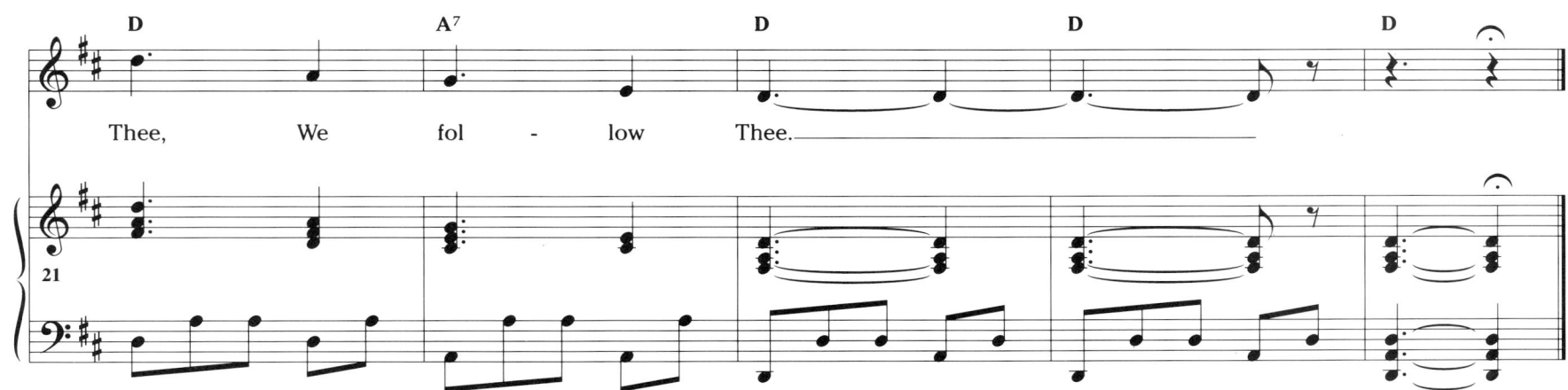

SHEET 3

**UNIT 1
A multi-faith song for assembly**

# Song of Light

1. (*mp*) See a light
   In the sky.
   O'er the world for all to see.
   Spark of light,
   Dark to bright,
   We are one, we look to Thee.

2. (*mf*) Hold the light
   Way up high.
   Feel its warmth and watch it glow.
   See the light
   Burning bright.
   Feed the flame and let it grow.

3. (*f*) Shine your light
   From within.
   Search for truth and charity.
   Hold my hand,
   Understand
   (*mf*<*f*>*mf*) We are one, we follow, follow Thee,
   We follow Thee.

**SHEET 1**

**A WORLD OF LIGHT** · SCHOFIELD & SIMS LTD   4

# Casting the Net

**UNIT 2**
**A play for assembly based on the Christian faith**

**CHARACTERS**
Jesus
Peter ⎫
James ⎪
John  ⎪
Philip ⎬ The Disciples
Andrew ⎪
Thomas ⎪
Nathanael ⎭

## Scene One

*It is the early hours of the morning and the seven disciples are casting their nets over the side of a boat on Lake Tiberias.*

**JAMES**

Nothing. Not one fish has swum into our net tonight. It is a waste of time.

**THOMAS**

It wasn't one of your best ideas, Peter. We've nothing to show for a full night's work.

**PETER** *angrily*

That's right. Blame me. All I said was that I was going fishing. You lot didn't have to come.

**ANDREW** *soothingly*

Peter's right. It's always been like this, you know that. Some nights we can hardly drag the nets home, they're so full and others are like tonight, nothing doing.

**PHILIP**

Well, I don't know much about fishing but I'd say if we haven't managed to catch any by now we're not likely to do so later on. Why don't we give up now and get back to the shore?

**PETER** *gloomily*

Yes, you're right. I've always caught something, though, in the past. It's the first time it's been a complete waste of time. Not even a couple of fish for our breakfasts. Oh, come on, then. Let's haul in the net and get back to dry land.

*They haul in the net and begin to row towards the shore.*

**JOHN**

Here comes sunrise. Look, there's somebody on the beach already — at this hour.

**NATHANAEL** *shading his eyes*

Must be another fisherman who's given up like us.

5   A WORLD OF LIGHT · SCHOFIELD & SIMS LTD

SHEET 1

# Casting the Net

**JAMES**

Mm. That fish smells good. He's got that from somewhere.

*He stands up in the boat and shouts.*

You've been luckier than us, friend. You've caught some fish, obviously.

**JESUS** *coming to the water's edge*

Young men, haven't you caught anything?

**NATHANAEL** *whispering to Philip*

He can't be much older than us and he calls us "young men".

**JOHN** *loudly*

We've been out all night and we haven't caught a thing.

**JESUS**

You will, if you throw your net on the right side of the boat instead of to your left. Why don't you try that?

**PETER** *wearily*

Oh, I'm tired now and we don't know if it will work.

**ANDREW**

We may as well try it. Come on, Thomas and Nathanael. It's your turn to row.

*They steer the boat round and row to the centre of the lake.*

## Scene Two

**PETER** *excitedly helping to drag in the net*

It's full to the top. I've never seen so many fish in one net in my life.

**PHILIP** *steadying the boat*

Be careful. You'll have us all over the side or you'll split the net. Take it easy.

**JOHN** *shading his eyes and peering towards the shore*

That man was right.

**JAMES** *pausing for a moment from dragging in the net*

Is he still there?

**JOHN**

Yes, he's waving to us. Oh, we should have known.

*He begins to wave excitedly.*

SHEET 2

A WORLD OF LIGHT · SCHOFIELD & SIMS LTD

# Casting the Net

**PETER** *sharply*

John, do you want to capsize us? Who is it?

**JOHN**

It's the Lord! We didn't recognise him. Oh, come on. Let's get to the shore.

**PETER** *leaping out of the boat*

The Lord? I'm coming, Lord, I'm coming.

**JOHN** *laughing*

Peter, for goodness sake, get your clothes on. Give him his cloak, Nathanael.

**ANDREW**

Isn't that just like Peter? He rushes off without a second thought. Go easy, James. We're almost there now.

**JOHN**

We haven't split the net. There must be over a hundred fish in there and the net won't need mending for a change.

**THOMAS**

It is the Lord, isn't it? It looks like him, but...

**PHILIP** *laughing*

Oh, Thomas, there you go again. Of course it's the Lord. Who else could it be?

**JAMES**

We'll soon find out. Come on. We'll leave the boat and the net here and wade the last few yards.

**JESUS** *as they approach*

Bring some of the fish with you. The fire is ready, as you see. Come and get yourselves warm.

**PETER**

You go to the fire. I'll get the fish.

*He hurries to the boat, returning with a handful of fish.*

7  A WORLD OF LIGHT · SCHOFIELD & SIMS LTD

SHEET 3

# Casting the Net

## Scene Three

*Jesus is cooking the fish and the seven disciples are sitting a few yards away, talking quietly.*

**ANDREW** *curiously*

Peter, what did you call the Lord when you saw him?

**PETER** *puzzled*

I called him "Lord". Why?

**JAMES**

Trust you to say the first thing that came into your head.

**PETER**

Why not? At least I gave him a welcome, which is more than you've all done. You seem shy and embarrassed.

**THOMAS**

Well, we are. I mean . . . the man looks like Jesus but . . . well, we all know what happened, and . . .

**PETER** *crossly*

And it isn't the first time he's come back to help us. He'll always see we have what we need. Even you should know that by now, Thomas.

**JESUS** *approaching with food*

If you won't come to sit near me, I'll have to bring the food to you. Come on, help yourselves. Bread and fish for everyone.

**JOHN** *taking the food*

I'm sorry, Lord, we didn't like to . . . well, we weren't sure if it was really you.

**JESUS** *smiling*

It's really me, John. Now, let's all move to the fire and enjoy being together for a little while.

*The disciples move close to Jesus and sit around him as they eat, talking quietly.*

# Jesus the Provider

**UNIT 2**
**A song for assembly based on the Christian faith**

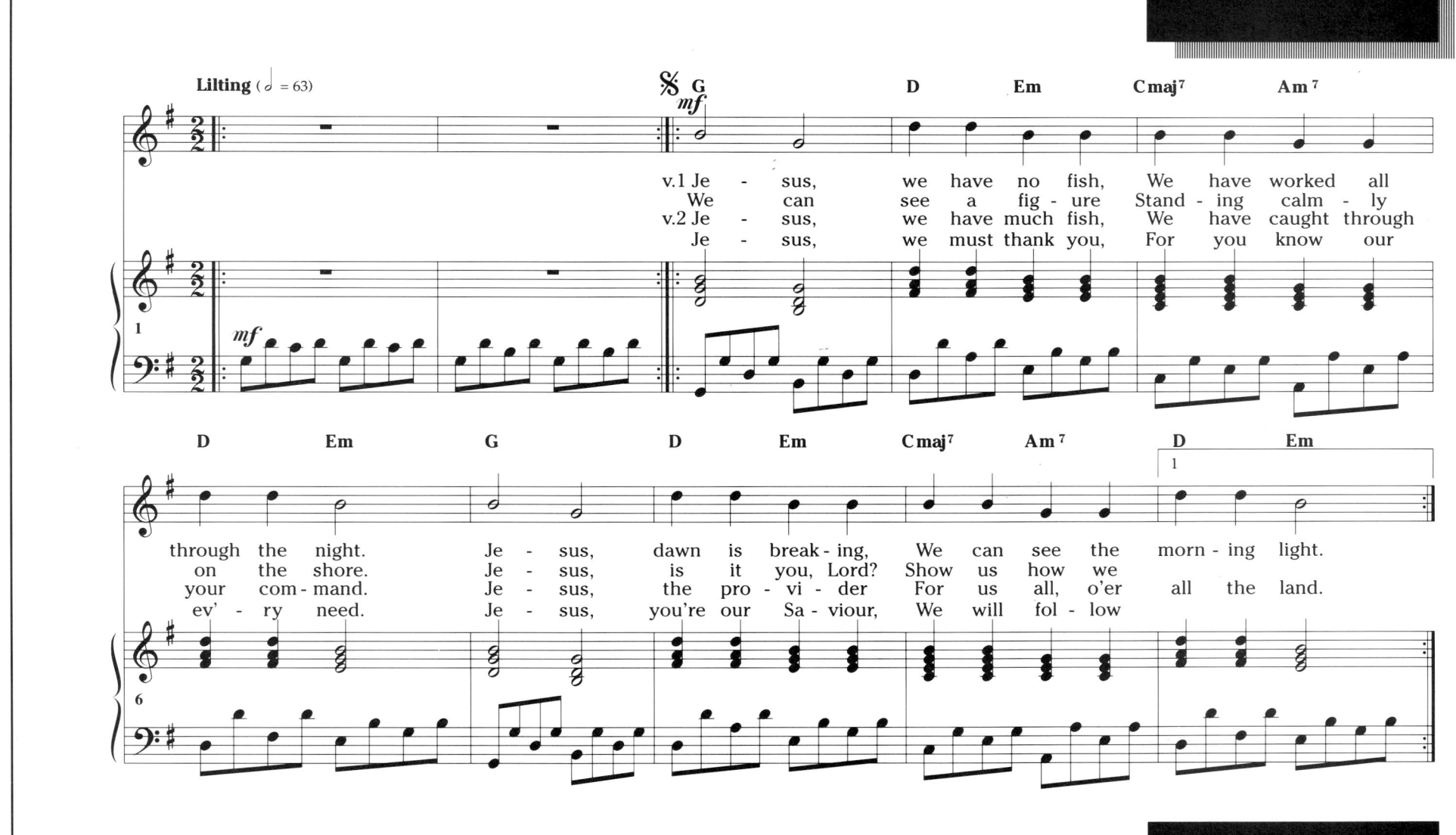

SHEET 1

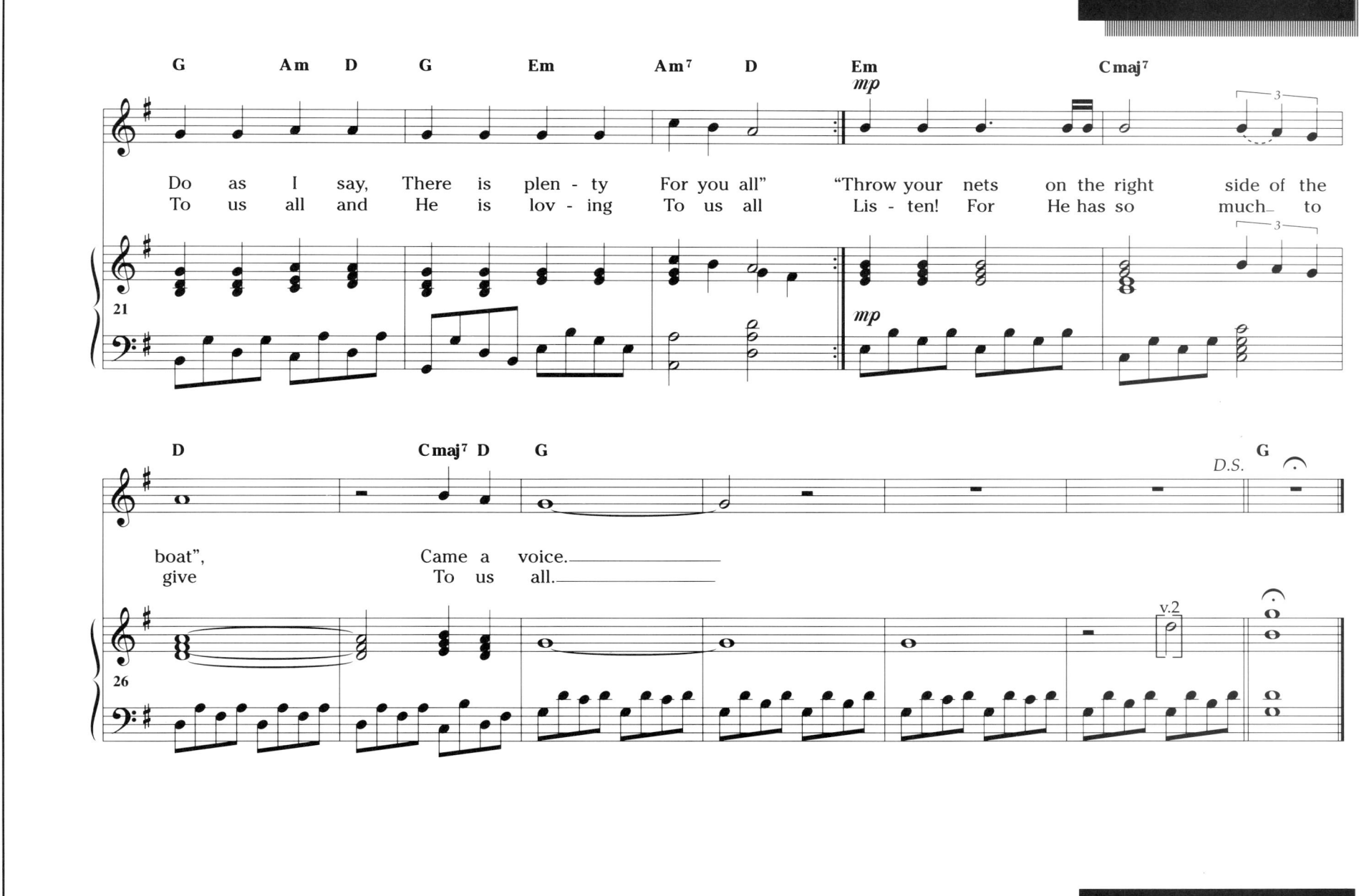

**UNIT 2**

**A song for assembly based on the Christian faith**

# Jesus the Provider

1. *(mf)* Jesus, we have no fish,
   We have worked all through the night.
   Jesus, dawn is breaking,
   We can see the morning light.
   We can see a figure
   Standing calmly on the shore.
   Jesus, is it you, Lord?
   Show us how we can catch more.

   *(mf)* "Throw your nets on the right side of the boat,"
   Came a voice that was calm and so remote.

   *(mf)* "Nets are empty,
   Do as I say,
   There is plenty
   For you all." } Repeat

   *(mp)* "Throw your nets on the right side of the boat,"
   Came a voice.

2. *(mf)* Jesus, we have much fish,
   We have caught through your command.
   Jesus the provider
   For us all, o'er all the land.
   Jesus, we must thank you,
   For you know our ev'ry need.
   Jesus, you're our Saviour,
   We will follow as you lead.

   *(mp)* Listen! For He has so much to give.
   *(mf)* Listen! For He has come that we may live.

   *(mf)* He is giving
   To us all and
   He is loving
   To us all. } Repeat
   Listen! For He has so much to give
   To us all.

**SHEET 1**

**A WORLD OF LIGHT** · SCHOFIELD & SIMS LTD

# The Guru and the Princes

**UNIT 3**

**A story for assembly based on the Sikh faith**

Guru Har Gobind was the sixth ruler of the Sikh faith and he lived in an area of North West India known as the Punjab during the seventeenth century. At that time, India was ruled by Muslim Emperors and the Emperor in Guru Har Gobind's leadership was called Jahangir.

Har Gobind's father was killed at the order of Emperor Jahangir and Har Gobind formed an army of Sikh soldiers who never actually fought but the Emperor was worried about them.

"There are two thousand of them," he told his ministers. "We'd better not harm Guru Har Gobind or any of his followers in case the soldiers attack us."

The Emperor began to invite Guru Har Gobind to his palace and take him on hunting trips. One day, Jahangir was attacked by a tiger and Guru Har Gobind saved his life. The two men might have become good friends but the Emperor wanted the whole of India to become Muslim and those who refused were killed or put in prison. The Guru did not agree with this and said so.

"I am going to throw that Guru into prison," Jahangir told his ministers. "People are listening to him and not to me."

"You can't," his ministers told him. "The people like him and if you imprison him the whole world will be against us."

The Emperor refused to listen. One day when Guru Har Gobind was sitting with his friends, Emperor Jahangir's men arrested him.

"You must not use violence. I shall be all right," Har Gobind told his army sternly. "Look after the rest of our people and protect them."

The soldiers had to watch helplessly as Har Gobind was led away. He was taken to an enormous fort in a town called Gwalior which everyone had forgotten about. It was a grey, dismal place and when the Guru arrived he was horrified to find fifty-two Hindu princes there, forgotten by the world and living in poor conditions with hardly any food and clothed in dirty rags they had been wearing for years.

"This is disgraceful," Har Gobind told the prison Governor angrily. "These men must be properly fed and clothed."

"Only you are to be fed well," answered the Governor, "by the Emperor's orders."

Guru Har Gobind shared all his food with the starving princes. They grew to trust him. He made so much fuss that the princes were, in the end, given clean clothes.

The Guru was in the fort for two years, and during that time other countries were arguing with the Emperor and sending letters to him.

"Other countries are beginning to hate us," the Emperor's ministers told him.

"There are letters every day demanding the release of Guru Har Gobind. Let him out or no one will have anything to do with us."

"And he saved your life," one of Jahangir's Government dared to say.

"And all those soldiers and followers stand outside the walls of the fort day and night shouting and wailing," another minister told the Emperor. "Set him free."

At first Jahangir refused but he saw that everyone was against him and, in the end, he sent a messenger to the fort to arrange for Guru Har Gobind's release.

"You are free to leave," the Governor told the Guru.

"No, thank you," replied the Guru politely. "I am staying here."

**A WORLD OF LIGHT · SCHOFIELD & SIMS LTD**

**SHEET 1**

# The Guru and the Princes

"What?" The Governor stared at him. "The Emperor orders you to leave."

"I am not going," said Guru Har Gobind firmly. "Not unless the princes go too."

"Ah, so that's it," said the Emperor when he heard. "Well, let him stay then. I've offered him his freedom and he doesn't want it. His request is impossible."

The Guru stayed, but again the protests came from all over the world. It was no use anyone saying that the Guru had been offered freedom. No one believed the Emperor. "Tell him he can take as many of the princes as can hold his hands as he walks out and no more," ordered the Emperor but still the Guru would not go.

"Tell him he can have anything else he wants but only the number of princes who can hold on to him may leave with him," ordered Jahangir.

"I agree," said the Guru, "on one condition."

"And what is that?" asked the Governor.

"I'd like a new suit of clothes, made exactly as I want it," replied the Guru and the Governor was pleased.

"Of course. I'll send in a tailor," he said and sent the tailor to tell the Emperor.

"Well, who would have thought a holy man could be so vain?," the Emperor said and could not stop laughing. "Tell the Governor to let the Guru have the new clothes and design them any way he wants," he told the tailor.

The Guru asked the tailor to sew fifty tapes on his clothes.

"They won't look very nice," she objected but the Guru replied that he had been told he could design his own outfit.

A few days later, the new clothes were ready. The Governor led him to the door of the prison. "I wish you had told us before that all you wanted was a new outfit," he said. "Now which of the princes are going with you?"

"As many as can hold on to me," answered Har Gobind.

Out of the shadowy passageways of the fort came fifty-two princes; all the prisoners held there for so many years. Fifty of them grasped the tapes on the Guru's clothes and two held his hands. Together they walked slowly out of the prison to the delighted welcome of the crowds.

Guru Har Gobind had led them all to safety.

# Hail, Har Gobind!

**UNIT 3 — A song for assembly based on the Sikh faith**

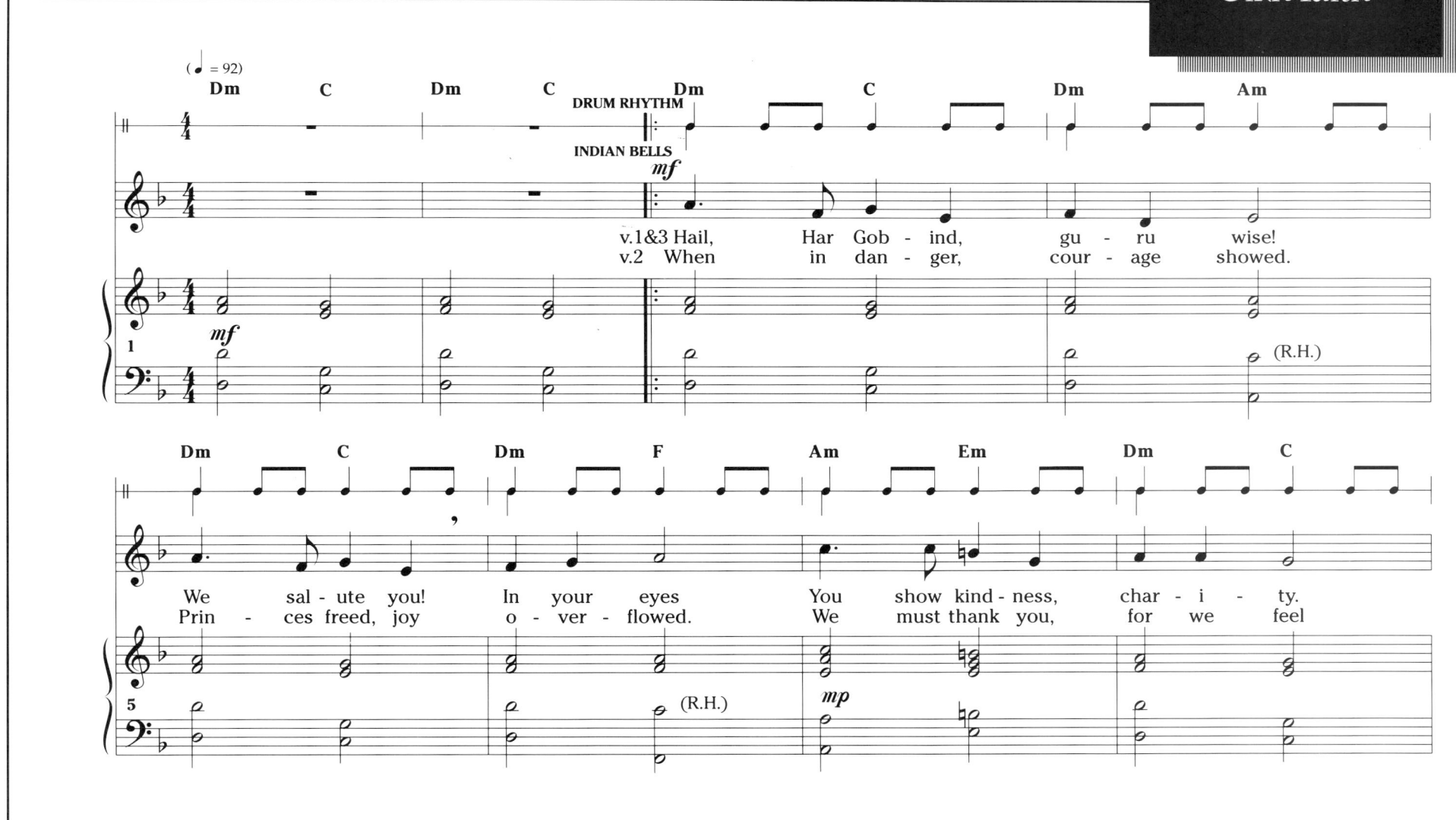

SHEET 1

# Hail, Har Gobind!

SHEET 2

# Hail, Har Gobind!

**UNIT 3**
**A song for assembly based on the Sikh faith**

1. *(mf)* Hail, Har Gobind, guru wise!
        We salute you! In your eyes
   *(mp)* You show kindness, charity.
        Man of wisdom, let us be
   *(mf)* Glad to know you, glad we can
        Be your friend, O loving man.

2. *(mf)* When in danger, courage showed.
        Princes freed, joy overflowed.
        We must thank you, for we feel
        Your great love for us is real.
        Glad to know you, glad we can
        Be your friend, O loving man.

3. *(mf)* Hail, Har Gobind, guru wise!
        We salute you! In your eyes
   *(mp)* You show kindness, charity.
        Man of wisdom, let us be
   *(mf)* Glad to know you, glad we can
        Be your friend, O loving man.

**SHEET 1**

**UNIT 4**

**A play for assembly based on the Jewish faith**

# Moses and the Princess

**CHARACTERS**
Eliezer, a teenager
Gershom, an elderly man
Rebekah, a girl
Jethro, a boy
Deborah, a girl
Phineas, a boy
Miriam, Moses' sister, aged about nine
Jochabed, mother of Moses
Princess, Pharaoh's daughter, in her early twenties
Girls, companions and servants of the princess — any number

*It is late afternoon in a desert town in Midian. A group of children are sitting in a circle around an elderly grey-haired man with a beard, and a boy in his mid-teens.*

**ELIEZER**

Uncle Gershom, are you really going home tomorrow? Why can't you and Phineas stay longer? You used to live here.

**GERSHOM**

I lived here when I was your age, Eliezer, yes, but I have only known a real home recently. As you know, most of my life has been spent wandering in the desert. I have to return to my family soon. Since this is the last time I can talk to you all on this visit, are there any stories you would like to hear again about your Great Uncle Moses?

**REBEKAH**

Tell us about Great Uncle Moses being put in a basket on the river, and how he was found by the princess and brought up as a prince.

**ELIEZER** *scornfully*

Uncle Gershom, the girls always want to hear that story. I like the one where Uncle Moses turned his stick into a snake and the magicians did the same.

**GERSHOM** *amused*

I will tell both stories. Close your eyes, children, and pretend that you see the fine country of Egypt with its tall, rich houses. Imagine the Pharaoh, who was stern and hard-hearted, telling his soldiers to go to all the Israelite homes and take all the baby boys down to the river and drown them. Which river was it?

**CHILDREN** *(in chorus)*

The Nile.

**GERSHOM**

Correct. Now we will travel to the poor quarters of Egypt, where the Israelites lived.

SHEET 1

**A WORLD OF LIGHT · SCHOFIELD & SIMS LTD    18**

# Moses and the Princess

We go to the home of a woman called Jochabed who is a member of the tribe of Levi. Jochabed is busy with something, as we shall see.

\* \* \*

## Scene One

*Early morning, in the home of Amram and Jochabed. It is a dark, poorly furnished room with a wooden table (centre) and a cradle (far left) where a baby is sleeping peacefully. Jochabed is placing a shawl in a large wicker basket which is on the table.*

**MIRIAM** *running in*

Mother, what is it? Why did you send for me? The overseer at the building site was really angry and said he would be coming to see you. Have the soldiers found out about the baby?

**JOCHABED** *sharply*

Keep your voice down or someone will hear you. Pick up the baby and give him to me.

*Miriam goes to the cradle and lifts the baby gently, talking softly to him. She hands him to her mother who hugs the child before putting him in the basket.*

**MIRIAM** *horrified*

Mother, what are you doing? He'll be frightened.

**JOCHABED** *sadly*

I'm afraid he will be when he wakes up but, hopefully, not for long. I want you to take the baby to the River Nile, to the spot where the princess bathes each day. Put the basket into the rushes by the Nile, and then hide for a while, and see what happens.

**MIRIAM** *doubtfully*

Mother, you saved him from the Nile and now you are putting him there yourself. He will be soaked inside the basket.

**JOCHABED**

No, he won't. I have made the basket waterproof by coating it with tar. Off you go, Miriam. I am relying on you.

# Moses and the Princess

**MIRIAM** *picking up the basket*

All right, Mother. Come on, little brother. We have an adventure ahead of us.

*She hurries out.*

**JOCHABED**

Oh, I hope I have done the right thing. He is so young, and so is Miriam, for all her grown up ways.

*She pulls a wooden stool to the table and covers her face with her hands, as the scene ends.*

## Scene Two

*An hour later, by the edge of the River Nile. (A backcloth of a river surrounded by trees and bushes.) Sounds of singing and laughter are heard and a pretty, richly dressed young woman, accompanied by a crowd of girls and young women of about her age, enters.*

**PRINCESS** *gaily*

Come on, someone, throw the ball. We must have our daily exercise.

*The girls begin to throw and chase a brightly coloured ball, shouting and laughing loudly. Suddenly, a piercing wail is heard, and the girls hear it and look at the princess.*

**PRINCESS**

Come on. Own up. Who made that dreadful noise?

*The wailing grows louder.*

**1st GIRL**

It wasn't us, your Highness. The noise came from over there.

*She points to the rushes by the river bank.*

**PRINCESS**

Go and see what it is, somebody, please.

**2nd GIRL** *fearfully*

It might be a wild animal, Highness.

**PRINCESS**

I don't think so. Well, if you are too afraid to investigate, I shall have to go myself.

*She hurries in the direction of the cries, which have now grown louder and, after searching in the rushes by the water's edge, holds up the basket in triumph.*

Here is your wild animal, girls.

SHEET 3

A WORLD OF LIGHT · SCHOFIELD & SIMS LTD  20

# Moses and the Princess

*She hurries back to the others with the basket, and the girls crowd round as the princess opens the basket. There are excited and also delighted cries from the girls as they see the baby. The princess picks up the baby and hugs him.*

**PRINCESS**

Don't be afraid, little one. You are safe now. Hush now. We'll soon have you warm and comfortable.

**1st GIRL**

What will you do with him, Highness?

**PRINCESS**

Do with him? Keep him, of course.

**1st GIRL**

But, Highness, you can't . . . your father . . .

**PRINCESS** *happily*

My father never refuses me anything. He won't mind.

**2nd GIRL**

Your Highness, look at the shawl in the basket. He is an Israelite child.

**PRINCESS** *calmly*

I know that. I saw the shawl too. An Israelite mother is trying to save her baby. Well, he shall be saved. I must find a nurse to take care of him for the time being. Then, when he is old enough, he can come to me at the palace and by then, my father will have forgotten his decree to kill all Israelite babies. One of you must go in search of a nurse.

**MIRIAM** *running out from behind a tree*

There is no need to look for a nurse, your Highness. I can find one for you at once, a good and loving woman who will look upon the baby as her own until you are ready to take him.

**PRINCESS**

You are an Israelite? Yes, of course you are, and you put the baby here, didn't you?

**MIRIAM**

I'd rather not say, your Highness.

**PRINCESS**

I understand. Well, fetch me this wonderful nurse now, please.

**MIRIAM** *joyfully*

Yes, your Highness.

*She curtseys to the Princess and goes out.*

**PRINCESS**

See, the child has stopped crying. He knows he is safe. I shall call him "Moses" because I

# Moses and the Princess

drew him from the water, and the name means that.

**MIRIAM** *hurrying in*

I met the nurse on the way to her house, Highness. She was only a short distance away.

**PRINCESS**

Come here, good woman. What is your name?

**JOCHABED** *nervously*

Jochabed, your Highness.

**PRINCESS**

Good. This child is to be called "Moses". Each week, someone from the palace will bring you money and receive a report on the baby's progress. He will stay with you for a few years until I send for him. Do you understand?

**JOCHABED**

Yes, your Highness.

**PRINCESS** *handing over the child*

Take good care of him. He is really Prince Moses.

*Jochabed takes the child in her arms and the princess hands her the shawl, which Jochabed wraps round the baby.*

**PRINCESS**

Rachel, go with them. Jochabed, you will do no work until the boy is returned to me. I will send a servant to you tomorrow with money, and he will see the overseer at your place of work.

*Jochabed nods and goes out with the baby, followed by Miriam.*

**3rd GIRL**

Highness, that woman was probably the child's real mother.

**PRINCESS**

Then the child could not be better cared for. Go on, Rachel. You are of Israelite descent. Go with them so that you can guide the servant there tomorrow. I want to know the kind of place in which my foster son will be living.

*Rachel hurries after Jochabed and Miriam as the scene fades.*

\* \* \*

SHEET 5

A WORLD OF LIGHT · SCHOFIELD & SIMS LTD  22

# Moses and the Princess

**GERSHOM**

And, as you all know, Moses did go to live in the palace, and Pharaoh's daughter adopted him. Prince Moses was brought up in the Royal Household, and might have stayed there, if, one day, he had not been sent to inspect one of the cities Pharaoh was making the Israelites build.

**ELIEZER**

And he saw an Egyptian overseer beating an Israelite, seized his whip, and killed the Egyptian.

**JETHRO**

And he ran out of Egypt, because Pharaoh was going to arrest him . . .

**REBEKAH**

On a charge of murder. And he came here to Midian and met Great Aunt Zipporah, and all our great grandmothers . . .

**JETHRO** *proudly*

And your grandfather, Uncle Gershom, whom I was called after.

**GERSHOM**

A very great man. My father was a shepherd here for many years and then God called him back to Egypt to rescue the Israelites.

**ELIEZER**

God called him through the burning bush. We know about that. It was when Great Uncle Moses was a shepherd, and he saw a bush on fire and heard God's voice calling him out of the bush.

**GERSHOM**

Do you remember what God said? Deborah, you are the youngest. Do you know?

**DEBORAH**

God said, "Take off your shoes, Moses, because you are on holy ground."

**GERSHOM** *pleased*

Good. Well, Moses went back to Egypt and he appeared before Pharaoh.

**PHINEAS**

That's where my grandfather came in. He went with Great Uncle Moses to Pharaoh and spoke for him, because Uncle Moses did not have a very strong voice.

**REBEKAH**

And then Pharaoh asked for a sign that Moses was sent by God.

**PHINEAS**

It was my grandfather, Aaron, who performed a miracle for Pharaoh, as you will see.

\* \* \*

# Moses and Aaron Beat The Magicians

**CHARACTERS**
Merneptah, King of Egypt, the Pharaoh
Moses
Aaron
Jannes — Pharaoh's magicians
Jambres
1st Official
2nd Official
3rd Official

*The scene takes place in Pharaoh's audience chamber, a large room in which the Pharaoh is sitting on a golden throne, surrounded by his officials.*

**PHARAOH** *impatiently*

Well? Was my order that the Israelites make bricks without straw obeyed?

**1st OFFICIAL**

It was obeyed, your Majesty, but the overseers had trouble enforcing it. It made those upstarts Moses and Aaron unpopular. The Israelites told them to go back where they came from.

**PHARAOH** *pleased*

Excellent. Then we can expect Moses and Aaron to be leaving us soon.

**2nd OFFICIAL**

No, your Majesty. They have no intention of giving up. They are requesting a further audience with you.

**PHARAOH**

Bring Jannes and Jambres to me at once.

*One of Pharaoh's officials goes out and returns almost at once with two magicians who bow before the king.*

**PHARAOH**

Jannes, Jambres. I have a test for you both and if you value your positions as court magicians, you had better do well. The two Israelites, Moses and Aaron, are still pestering me to allow them to take their people into the wilderness to make a supposed sacrifice. Obviously, I have no intention of allowing that but, once and for all, I wish to show them to be the foolish men they are. I am going to ask them to perform a miracle of magic for me. I hope you are both equal to any tests they may be asked to perform.

**JANNES** *bowing*

We won't fail you, your Majesty.

**JAMBRES**

Whatever you ask them to do, we will match them in skill, your Majesty.

**PHARAOH**

Tell the Israelites to come before the King.

*Moses and Aaron are brought before Pharaoh, and they bow to him respectfully.*

SHEET 7

A WORLD OF LIGHT · SCHOFIELD & SIMS LTD

# Moses and Aaron Beat The Magicians

**PHARAOH** *bored*

What is it this time, Aaron? Haven't I made my answers to your requests plain enough?

**AARON** *politely*

We thought you may have reconsidered, your Majesty. Our request is the same as before.

**PHARAOH**

Does this God of yours give you the power to perform miracles?

**AARON** *quietly*

Why, your Majesty, I hadn't thought about it but I expect He does.

**PHARAOH**

Perform one, then.

**AARON**

Very well, your Majesty.

*He throws his stick on the ground and the officials cry out as it turns into a snake, wriggling on the floor.*

**PHARAOH** *sharply*

Jannes, Jambres, can you better that?

**JANNES** *confidently*

Of course, your Majesty.

*He and Jambres throw down their sticks which also turn into snakes.*

**PHARAOH** *delighted*

Well, your God can't beat my magicians. If he could, I would release your Israelites at once.

**AARON**

Would you, Pharaoh?

*He and the assembled group watch as Aaron's snake swallows the snakes of the other magicians.*

**MOSES** *softly*

So is the power of our God greater than the power of your magicians?

**PHARAOH**

Do something, Jannes and Jambres.

**JAMBRES** *scared*

We can't beat that, your Majesty.

SHEET 8

## Moses and Aaron Beat The Magicians

**PHARAOH** *bitterly*

So you have failed me. Moses, Aaron, it makes no difference. I have no intention of releasing the Israelites, not now or at any other time. Show them out, please, someone.

*He waves them away and Moses and Aaron go out.*

\* \* \*

**GERSHOM**

But, as you all know, Pharaoh was, in the end, forced to release the Israelites because the power of God was too great for him and his people. Moses, my father, led the Israelites into the wilderness. They were wild and undisciplined and they often gave him a hard time, I remember. I was born and grew up in the wilderness, and my father's heart was often heavy, because of the behaviour of the people. He walked always with God and he gave to all of us the laws of God. From the wild, unruly crowds came a great nation, the chosen nation, the chosen nation which will last forever, one founded by my father, God's true and fearless prophet. Our people have endured much but they will always, in the end, return to the Promised Land to which God called them and will always call them. Sing now of Moses, my children. May the light which led this wonderful man, the true light of God, shine forever in your hearts.

# Moses

**UNIT 4**
**A song for assembly based on the Jewish faith**

27  A WORLD OF LIGHT · SCHOFIELD & SIMS LTD

SHEET 1

# Moses

SHEET 2

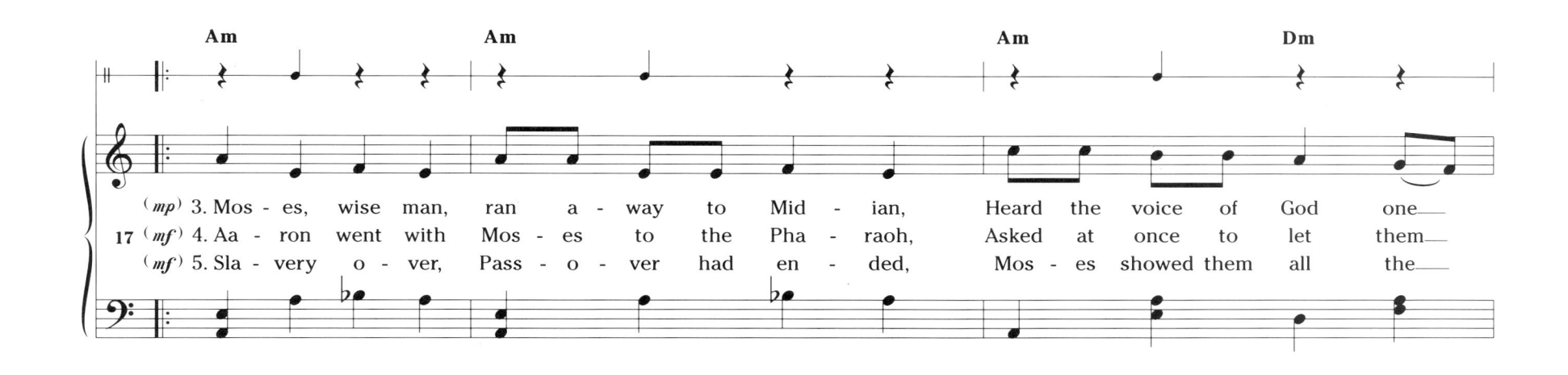

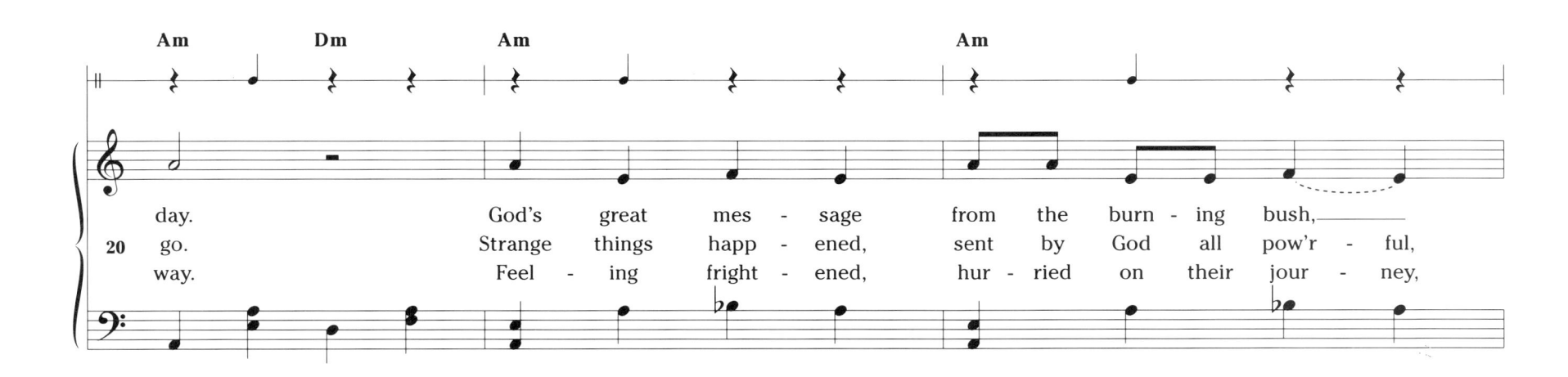

# Moses

(mp) 3. Mos - es, wise man, ran a - way to Mid - ian, Heard the voice of God one
(mf) 4. Aa - ron went with Mos - es to the Pha - raoh, Asked at once to let them
(mf) 5. Sla - very o - ver, Pass - o - ver had en - ded, Mos - es showed them all the

day. God's great mes - sage from the burn - ing bush,
go. Strange things happ - ened, sent by God all pow'r - ful,
way. Feel - ing fright - ened, hur - ried on their jour - ney,

29  A WORLD OF LIGHT · SCHOFIELD & SIMS LTD

SHEET 3

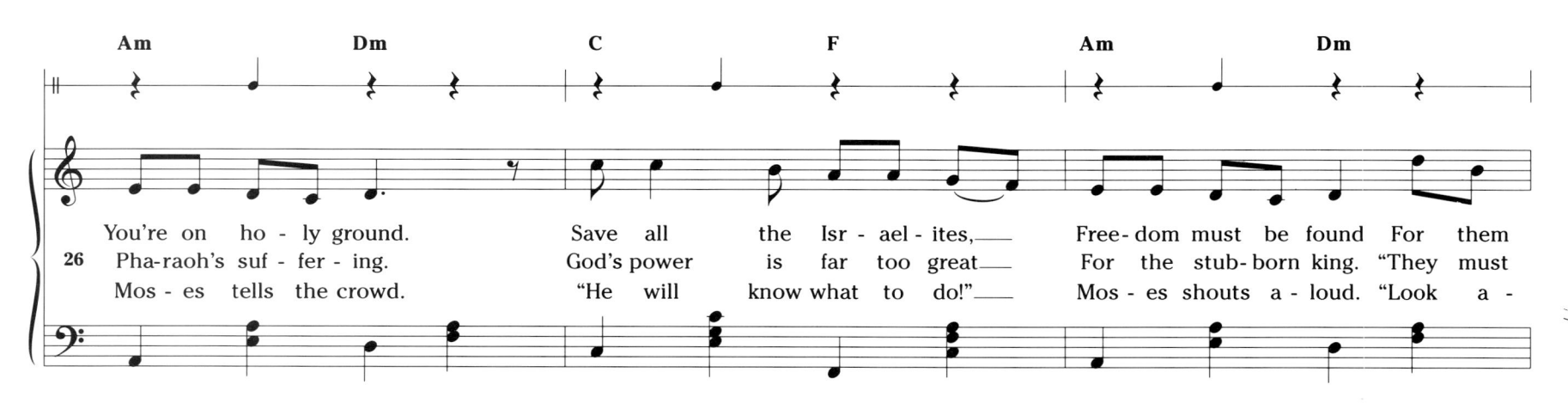

# Moses

| Am | Dm | Am | Dm | CHORUS C | F |

23  
Mos - es heard what God had to say. *(mf)* "Take off your shoes, Mos - es,  
Pha - raoh did - n't want to know. *(f)* God's send - ing plagues, Mos - es,  
Pha - raoh's men not far a - way! *(f)* "The Lord will fight for you!" —

| Am | Dm | C | F | Am | Dm |

26  
You're on ho - ly ground. Save all the Isr - ael - ites, — Free - dom must be found For them  
Pha - raoh's suf - fer - ing. God's power is far too great — For the stub - born king. "They must  
Mos - es tells the crowd. "He will know what to do!" — Mos - es shouts a - loud. "Look a -

SHEET 4

# Moses

# Moses

Waters closing! Pha-raoh's men were drown-ing, Thanks be to our God's guid-ing Hand.

Lead, di-rect us, keep us and pro-tect us, Shine with-in our hearts a-new, a-new.

SHEET 6

A WORLD OF LIGHT · SCHOFIELD & SIMS LTD  32

# Moses

**UNIT 4**
**A song for assembly based on the Jewish faith**

1. (*mf*) Moses, baby, taken to the river,
   Hidden from the cruel Pharaoh's men.
   Princess named him, drew him from the water,
   Brought him back to safety then.

2. (*mp*) Moses, young man, living in the palace,
   Went to see a city one day.
   (*mf*) Saw an Egyptian beat a man from Israel,
   Moses killed him right away.

   CHORUS
   (*f*) Run off to Midian, Moses,
   Pharaoh's after you!
   Go there and guard the sheep.
   God will speak to you.
   Off you go!

3. (*mp*) Moses, wise man, ran away to Midian,
   Heard the voice of God one day.
   God's great message from the burning bush,
   Moses heard what God had to say.

   CHORUS
   (*mf*) "Take off your shoes, Moses,
   You're on holy ground.
   Save all the Israelites,
   Freedom must be found
   For them all."

4. (*mf*) Aaron went with Moses to the Pharaoh,
   Asked at once to let them go.
   Strange things happened, sent by God all pow'rful,
   Pharaoh didn't want to know.

   CHORUS
   (*f*) God's sending plagues, Moses,
   Pharaoh's suffering.
   God's power is far too great
   For the stubborn king.
   "They must go!"

33  A WORLD OF LIGHT · SCHOFIELD & SIMS LTD

SHEET 1

# Moses

5. *(mf)* Slavery over, Passover had ended,
   Moses showed them all the way.
   Feeling frightened, hurried on their journey,
   Pharaoh's men not far away!

   *(f)* CHORUS
   "The Lord will fight for you!"
   Moses tells the crowd.
   "He will know what to do!"
   Moses shouts aloud.
   "Look ahead!"

6. *(mf)* Sea waves parted, showed them all the way to
   Travel safely to the Promised Land.
   Waters closing! Pharaoh's men were drowning,
   Thanks be to our God's guiding Hand.

7. *(f)* Moses, prophet, may the true bright light,
   Given by our gracious God to you.
   Lead, direct us, keep us and protect us,
   Shine within our hearts anew, anew.

SHEET 2

# The Wise and Foolish Bridesmaids

**UNIT 5**
**A play for assembly based on the Christian faith**

### CHARACTERS
Elizabeth
Deborah
Judith
Hannah
Miriam
Tabitha
Rachel
Ruth
Sarah
Susannah
Marcus, the bridegroom
Steward

### INTRODUCTION

If I were to ask how many of you have been to a wedding, I'm sure almost every hand would be raised. Perhaps some of you boys have been page boys at an older sister or aunty's wedding.

I'm going to ask the girls a question this morning. Have any of you ever been bridesmaids? If you have, you'll remember the excitement of trying on your dress beforehand and on the day itself, and of following the bride to her wedding, either up the aisle in a church or to the Registry Office.

It was exactly the opposite in the time of Jesus, two thousand years ago. The bridesmaids led the bridegroom to his wedding. The girls, dressed in beautiful clothes would wait in the bridegroom's house or the home of a relative, and the bridegroom could arrive at any time for his wedding during the evening. Sometimes it might be midnight when he arrived and the girls would lead him through the dark streets, carrying oil lamps to light the way to the bride's house. No girl would be allowed to lead the bridegroom unless her lamp was lit. Once the door had closed on the last of the bridesmaids, no-one else was allowed in.

Jesus likened himself to a bridegroom. He wanted everyone to be ready because no one knows when the lives we are living will end.

## Scene One

*In a room at the bridegroom Marcus' house in Jerusalem. The bridesmaids are resting on long couches on either side of the stage, their lamps on a table between them.*

**TABITHA** *yawning*

It's getting late. I wonder what time Marcus will come.

**JUDITH** *sleepily*

I don't know but I'm going to have a sleep now. We'll hear Marcus when he arrives.

**RUTH** *examining her lamp*

I hope the oil holds out.

35  A WORLD OF LIGHT · SCHOFIELD & SIMS LTD

SHEET 1

# The Wise and Foolish Bridesmaids

**ELIZABETH** *surprised*

Didn't you bring any extra oil with you?

**RUTH** *cheerfully*

No. I didn't think of it.

**MIRIAM**

The shops are still open. Why don't you go for some? Better to be safe than sorry.

**RUTH**

I can't be bothered. Anyway, I'm not going out into the street by myself at this time of night.

**MIRIAM** *to everyone*

Who else hasn't brought any extra oil?

**JUDITH** *yawning*

I haven't.

**DEBORAH & SUSANNAH** *(together)*

I haven't either.

**TABITHA**

I forgot all about it. I was in a hurry.

**ELIZABETH**

Well, why don't you all go and get some? You can look after each other.

**TABITHA** *crossly*

Don't order us about, Elizabeth. We'll do as we like.

**DEBORAH**

It's a long way to the shops. Marcus might come and we'll miss him.

**SARAH**

You could be there and back in no time. Don't think you'll have any of our oil if your lamps go out.

**SUSANNAH** *sharply*

We wouldn't expect to get any from you, Sarah.

**MIRIAM** *quietly*

If you're not going out we should all try to rest. The celebrations go on all night, remember.

*The girls lie down again on the couches.*

SHEET 2

A WORLD OF LIGHT · SCHOFIELD & SIMS LTD  36

## The Wise and Foolish Bridesmaids

**ELIZABETH**

Sarah?

**SARAH** *jumping up*

What? Is Marcus coming?

**ELIZABETH** *anxiously*

Supposing their lamps do go out. What then?

**SARAH** *impatiently*

It's up to each one of us to be ready when a bridegroom comes. We all know that. If they can't be bothered to bring extra oil or go and buy it, that's their business. Rest, Elizabeth.

**ELIZABETH**

We haven't enough to give them any?

**SARAH**

Of course we can't. You are too kind, Elizabeth.

**ELIZABETH** *sighing*

I suppose you're right.

*They rest and the lights are dimmed.*

## Scene Two

*In the same house, an hour later.*

**VOICE** *outside*

The bridegroom has arrived. Are you ready, girls?

**MIRIAM**

Wake up everyone. Get your lamps. Marcus has come for us.

**VOICE** *outside*

Bring your lamps and come out, bridesmaids. The groom is waiting.

**RUTH** *dismayed*

My lamp's gone out. Oh, no.

**DEBORAH**

Mine's gone out, too.

---

37    A WORLD OF LIGHT · SCHOFIELD & SIMS LTD     SHEET 3

# The Wise and Foolish Bridesmaids

**TABITHA**

And mine. And yours, Judith.

**JUDITH**

Everyone's lamp has gone out. The trouble is that we five haven't any extra oil and the others have.

**RUTH**

What are we going to do? They won't lend us any oil.

**ELIZABETH**

We would if we could but we've only enough for ourselves. Go to the shop and get some.

**TABITHA**

Come on. It's the only thing we can do. The steward won't let us lead Marcus with no oil in our lamps.

*She leads the way out left.*

**SARAH** *loudly*

We're coming, Steward. Are you ready, girls?

**HANNAH**

Does my lamp look all right?

**SARAH**

Yes, it's fine. Come on, now. Lead the way, Miriam. Oh, do stop banging, Steward. We're here.

**STEWARD** *entering*

I thought there were ten of you. Where are the others?

**ELIZABETH**

They'll be here in a minute, Steward.

**STEWARD** *impatiently*

Where are they?

**HANNAH** *timidly*

They've gone to the shop for more oil.

**STEWARD**

At this hour? They'll be gone for ages. We must go.

**ELIZABETH & RACHEL** *(together)*

Oh, please wait for them.

**STEWARD**

Certainly not. If you girls could remember to bring extra oil, so could they. No. You five will have to light the way for Marcus – but it's really not good enough.

SHEET 4

A WORLD OF LIGHT · SCHOFIELD & SIMS LTD   38

# The Wise and Foolish Bridesmaids

**MIRIAM**

Let's hope they catch us up.

**STEWARD**

Well, if they do that's all right, but they'll have to hurry. Come along now. The bridegroom has waited long enough.

*They go out.*

## Scene Three

*Outside the house where the wedding is being held. Sounds of music are coming from a door (back centre).*

**JUDITH** *holding up her lamp*

Where are the others? I was sure they'd wait for us.

**RUTH** *upset*

Perhaps the steward wouldn't let them wait. We'd better knock.

**TABITHA** *knocking on the door*

Let us in. Can you hear us?

**STEWARD** *opening door*

Yes? What do you want?

**JUDITH**

We're the other bridesmaids. We've come to the wedding.

**STEWARD**

I'm afraid the bridesmaids have arrived. The festivities have begun.

**RUTH**

But . . . but we should be there.

**STEWARD**

Yes, perhaps you should but you were not ready when the bridegroom came. You know the rules by now.

**TABITHA**

Oh, please . . . please let us in. We'll be very quiet.

39  A WORLD OF LIGHT · SCHOFIELD & SIMS LTD

SHEET 5

## The Wise and Foolish Bridesmaids

**STEWARD** *firmly*

No. It's against the rules. You had your chances. Off you go, now. You only have yourselves to blame.

*He closes the door with a bang as the girls walk dejectedly away.*

SHEET 6

# Be Prepared

**UNIT 5
A song for assembly based on the Christian faith**

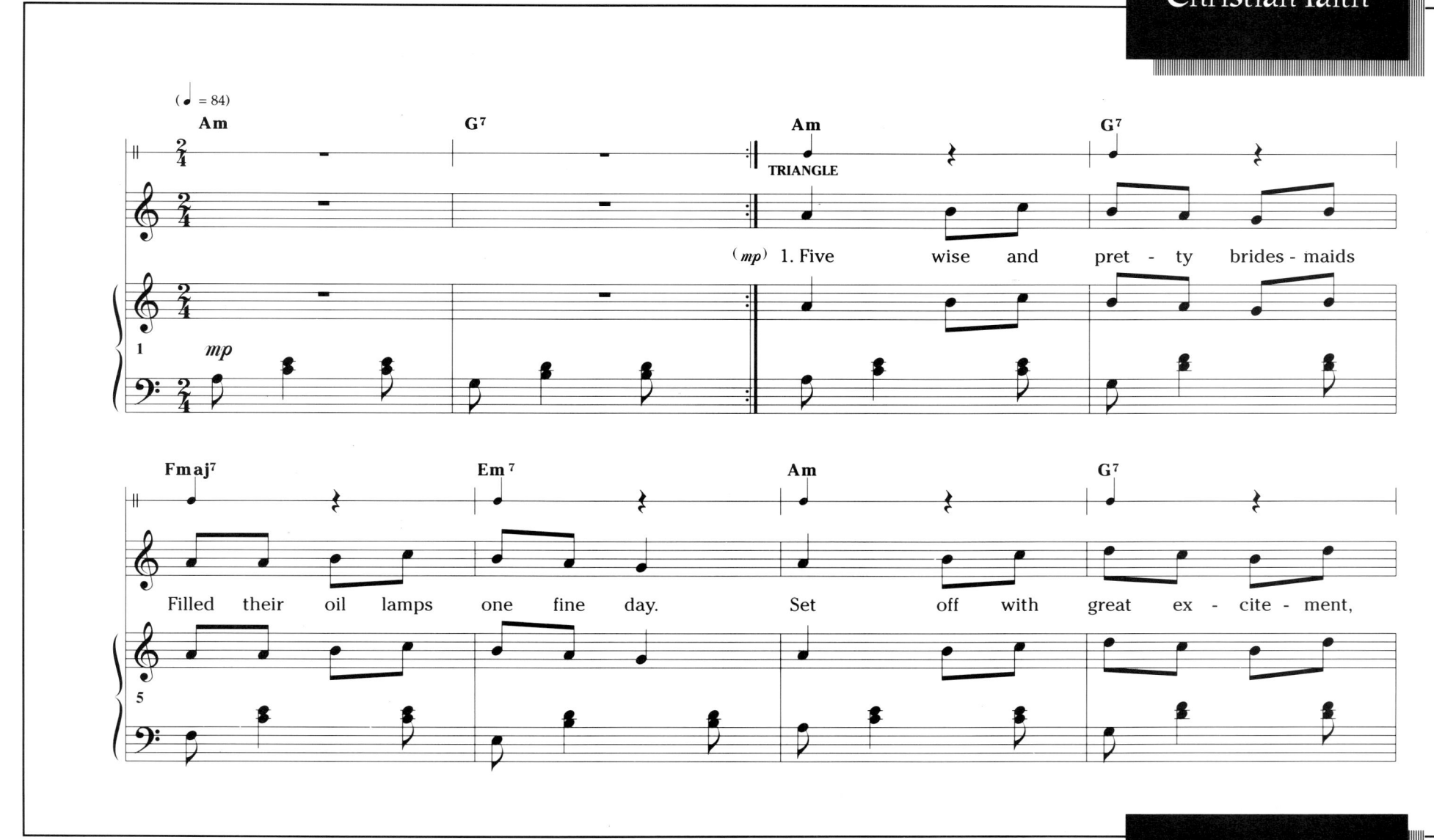

1. Five wise and pretty bridesmaids
Filled their oil lamps one fine day.
Set off with great excitement,

SHEET 1

A WORLD OF LIGHT · SCHOFIELD & SIMS LTD

# Be Prepared

For the groom was on his way. (*mf*) 2. Five foolish pretty brides-maids

Took half empty lamps that day. Set off with great excitement,

SHEET 2

A WORLD OF LIGHT · SCHOFIELD & SIMS LTD  42

Am7 G7 F C
TAMBOURINE
For the groom was on his way. (mf) 3. Bride - groom late, the
17
Dm7 Fmaj7 G F C
ten laid down to rest, When mid - night came, a
21

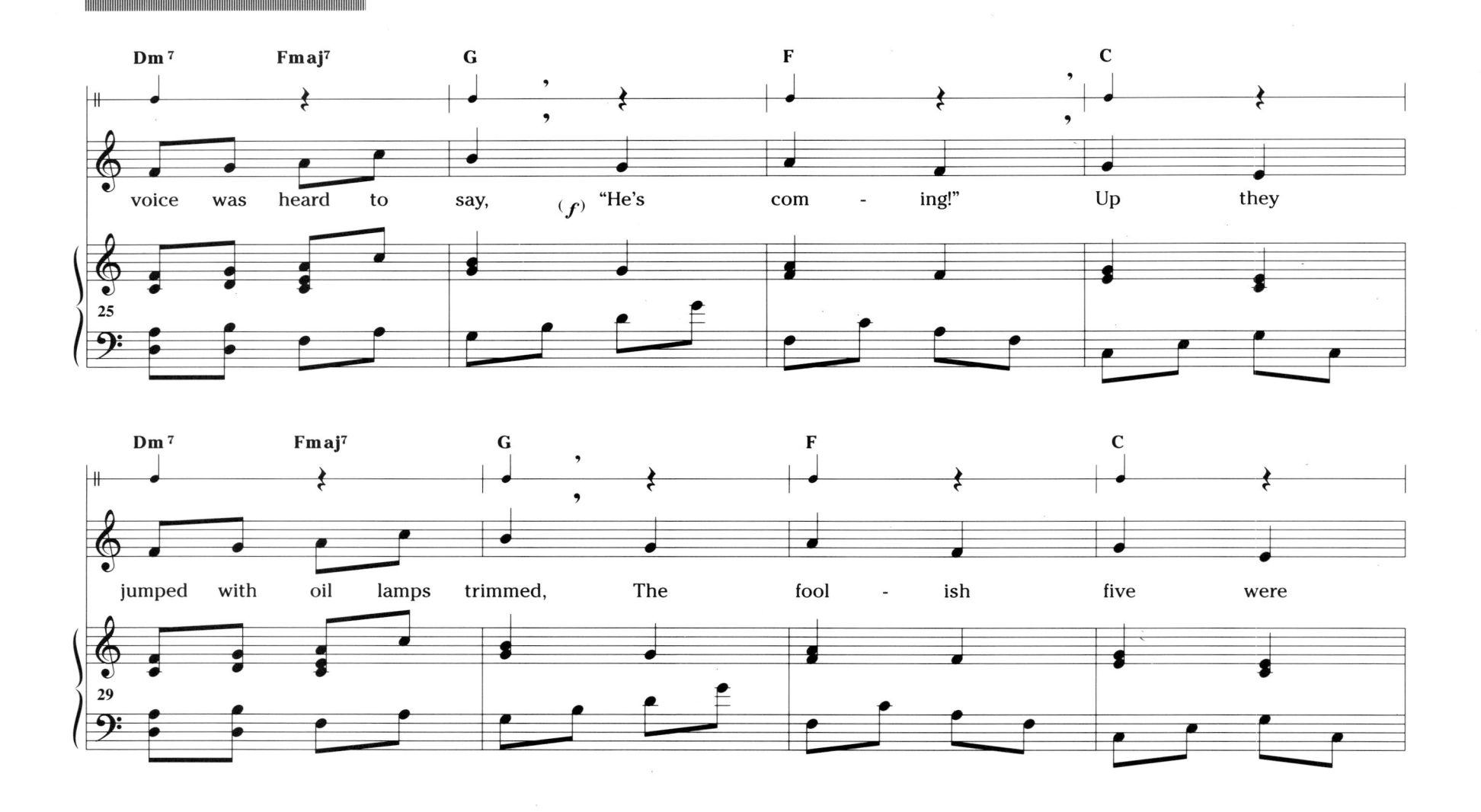

# Be Prepared

voice was heard to say, (*f*) "He's com-ing!" Up they jumped with oil lamps trimmed, The fool-ish five were

SHEET 4

A WORLD OF LIGHT · SCHOFIELD & SIMS LTD    44

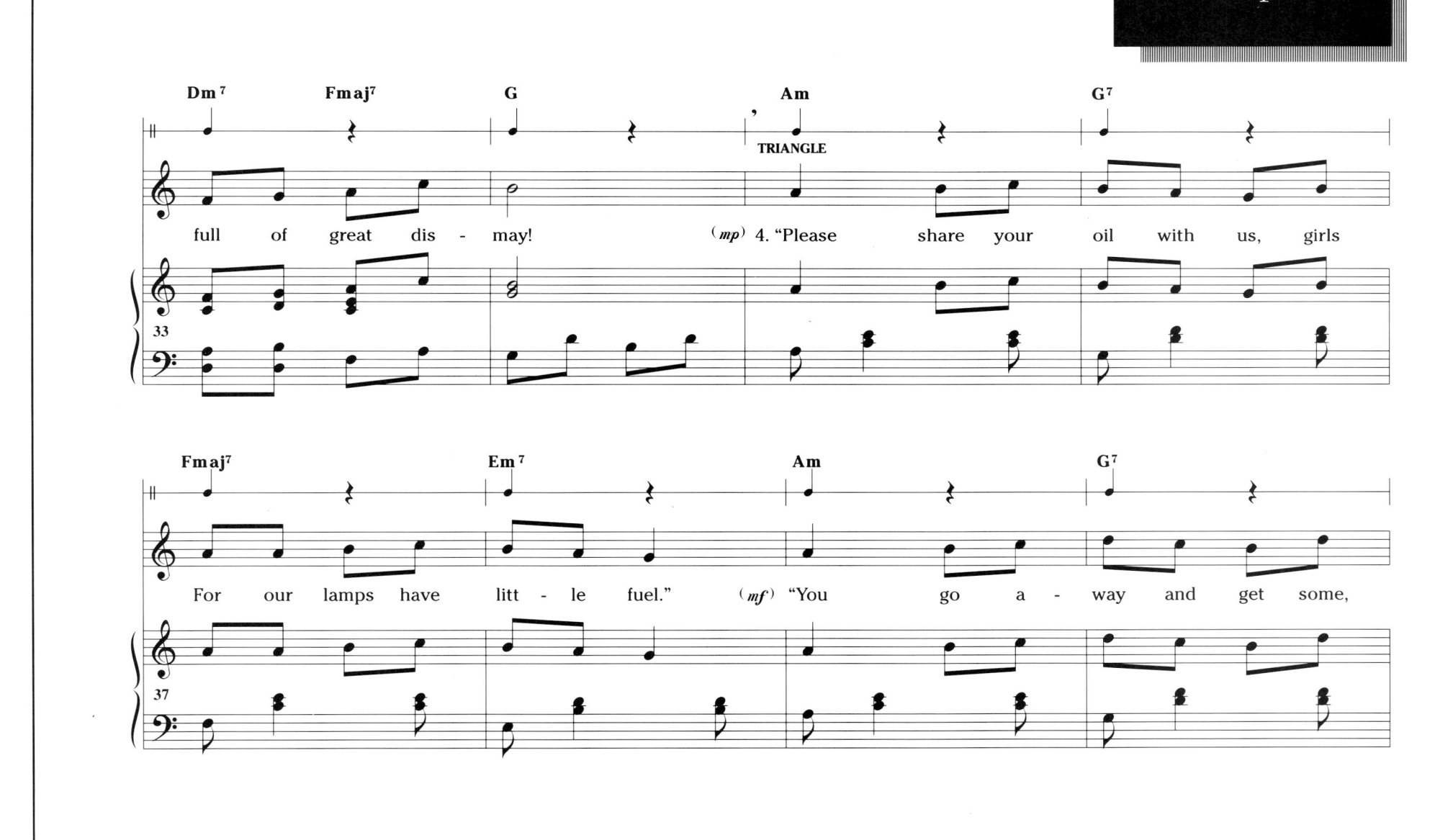

# Be Prepared

full of great dis - may! *(mp)* 4. "Please share your oil with us, girls

For our lamps have litt - le fuel." *(mf)* "You go a - way and get some,

45  A WORLD OF LIGHT · SCHOFIELD & SIMS LTD

SHEET 5

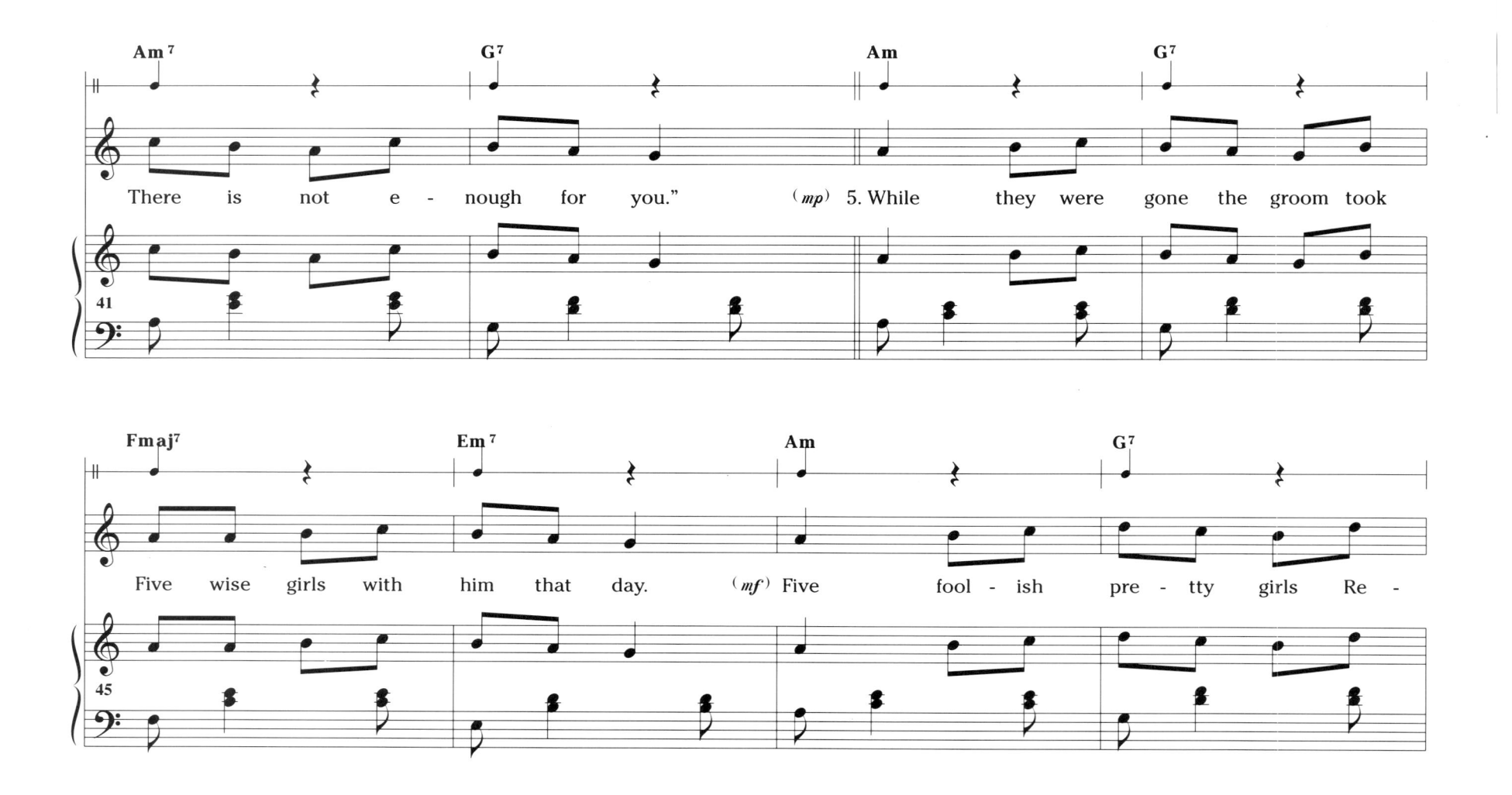

# Be Prepared

There is not e-nough for you." *(mp)* 5. While they were gone the groom took Five wise girls with him that day. *(mf)* Five fool-ish pre-tty girls Re-

SHEET 6

A WORLD OF LIGHT · SCHOFIELD & SIMS LTD   46

# Be Prepared

turned too late, were turned a-way. (*mf*) 6. "Be pre-pared," said

Jes-us to his faith-ful, "Wait, hear, act up-

# Be Prepared

on your God's com - mands, Then you'll be read - y for your heav'n - ly king - dom, Meet your God, your lives are in His hands."

# Be Prepared

**UNIT 5**
**A song for assembly based on the Christian faith**

1. *(mp)* Five wise and pretty bridesmaids
   Filled their oil lamps one fine day.
   Set off with great excitement,
   For the groom was on his way.

2. *(mf)* Five foolish pretty bridesmaids
   Took half-empty lamps that day.
   Set off with great excitement,
   For the groom was on his way.

3. *(mf)* Bridegroom late, the ten laid down to rest,
   When midnight came, a voice was heard to say,
   "He's coming!" Up they jumped with oil lamps trimmed,
   The foolish five were full of great dismay!

4. *(mp)* "Please share your oil with us, girls
   For our lamps have little fuel."
   *(mf)* "You go away and get some,
   There is not enough for you."

5. *(mp)* While they were gone the groom took
   Five wise girls with him that day.
   *(mf)* Five foolish pretty girls
   Returned too late, were turned away.

6. *(mf)* "Be prepared," said Jesus to his faithful.
   "Wait, hear, act upon your God's commands.
   Then you'll be ready for your heav'nly kingdom,
   Meet your God, your lives are in his hands."

**A WORLD OF LIGHT** · SCHOFIELD & SIMS LTD

SHEET 1

## UNIT 6
### A story for assembly based on the Islamic faith

# The Thirsty Dog

**INTRODUCTION**

*The Holy Prophet Muhammad, the last of a long line of prophets of Islam, was especially fond of animals. Once, when a tired dog lay on his cloak with her puppies, he cut his cloak in two so that he would not have to disturb the weary mother dog. He told the following story to his friends because he wanted them to know how God wished them to behave to all God's creatures.*

Malik had been travelling by camel through the desert since early morning and by midday he was tired and thirsty. The only well he had found was dry and that was hours ago.

"Surely there must be a well or a water hole somewhere," he muttered to himself, wiping the dust from his eyes with a weary hand. "Oh why did I leave my water bag behind?"

The day wore on and, finally, Malik could go no further. The camel needed to rest too, because they had many kilometres to go before darkness fell.

"All right, friend. You can let me off now," he croaked to the tired animal who obediently sank down into the sand to allow Malik to slide from its back.

With sore eyes and a parched throat, Malik went in search of water. A dark object in the distance had caught his attention. It was probably an old cattle trough used by the nomads but he felt he should make sure.

It was a well and Malik knelt down and gave thanks to God. It was a miracle.

He remembered that the well might be empty and he picked up a small stone and threw it into the dark depths of the well shaft. A soft splash told him that there was definitely water in there and he began to search for the bucket which was usually attached to a well.

There was no bucket to be found anywhere. There was cool, clear water in the well but there was no way that Malik could get to it. He leaned over the well shaft and felt along its sides. There were small ridges on either side and Malik knew that he would have to use these to climb down to the water, which seemed to be a very long way off.

"What will I hold on to ?" he wondered.

He remembered that he had a coil of rope in his luggage and he hurried back to the camel and found the rope. He returned to the well and fastened one end of the rope to one of the well supports as securely as possible. He was just about to climb into the well shaft, thinking he had solved the problem, when he remembered that he had nothing to put the water in.

Malik removed one of his sandals and a leather sock. He replaced the sandal, put the sock between his teeth and, gripping the rope tightly, he climbed into the well shaft.

It was a long and difficult journey down to the water. The sides of the well were wet and slippery and Malik might have fallen many times if he had not had the rope to hold.

At last he found himself just above the level of the water. He took one hand from the rope, removed the sock from between his teeth and bent down to fill the sock. He twisted the open end of the sock tightly and put the twisted end in his mouth again.

The journey back to the top of the well was even more dangerous and Malik almost fell out of the shaft at the other end. He was

SHEET 1

# The Thirsty Dog

exhausted, even too tired to open the sock and drink the water.

At last he reached for the sock and was about to have a much needed drink when he heard a sound.

He looked round and saw an old desert dog crawling towards him.

The dog was thin and ill and his tongue was hanging out. He looked at Malik with pleading eyes.

Malik sighed wearily and put the sock beside the thirsty dog, who drank until there was no water left.

Malik left the sock with the dog, removed his other sock and, with a heavy sigh, began the dangerous journey once again. As he climbed into the well shaft, the dog sat and watched for a while and then, feeling much better, crept quietly away. Malik made the second journey safely and at last had his long drink of fresh water.

"He will be greatly blessed by God," Muhammad told his followers. "God loves all animals and wants you to do the same."

## UNIT 6
### A song for assembly based on the Islamic faith

# The Thirsty Dog

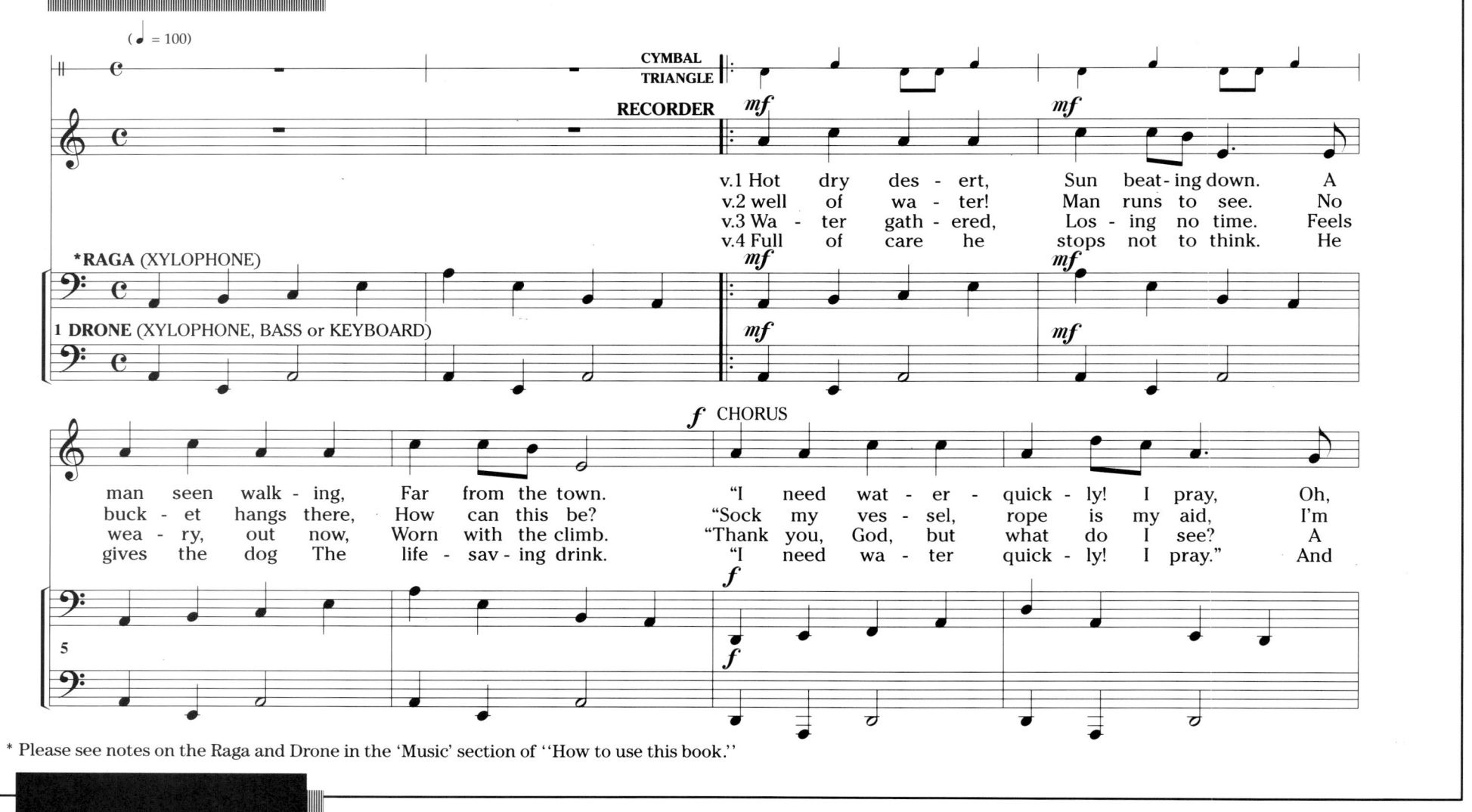

($\quarter = 100$)

**CYMBAL**
**TRIANGLE**

**RECORDER** *mf* *mf*

v.1 Hot dry des - ert, Sun beat - ing down. A
v.2 well of wa - ter! Man runs to see. No
v.3 Wa - ter gath - ered, Los - ing no time. Feels
v.4 Full of care he stops not to think. He

***RAGA** (XYLOPHONE)* *mf* *mf*

**1 DRONE** (XYLOPHONE, BASS or KEYBOARD) *mf* *mf*

*f* **CHORUS**

man seen walk - ing, Far from the town. "I need wat - er quick - ly! I pray, Oh,
buck - et hangs there, How can this be? "Sock my ves - sel, rope is my aid, I'm
wea - ry, out now, Worn with the climb. "Thank you, God, but what do I see? A
gives the dog The life - sav - ing drink. "I need wa - ter quick - ly! I pray." And

*f*

\* Please see notes on the Raga and Drone in the 'Music' section of "How to use this book."

**SHEET 1**

A WORLD OF LIGHT · SCHOFIELD & SIMS LTD    52

# The Thirsty Dog

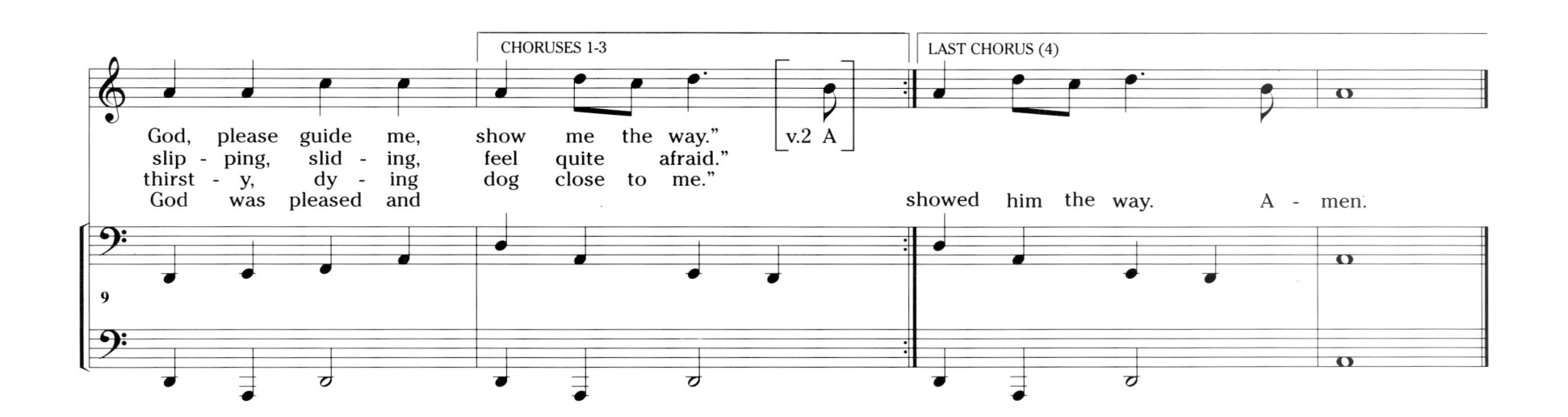

CHORUSES 1-3 | LAST CHORUS (4)

God, please guide me, show me the way."
slip - ping, slid - ing, feel quite afraid."
thirst - y, dy - ing dog close to me."
God was pleased and showed him the way. A - men.

v.2 A

53  **A WORLD OF LIGHT** · SCHOFIELD & SIMS LTD

SHEET 2

**UNIT 6**
**A song for assembly based on the Islamic faith**

# The Thirsty Dog

1. (*mf*) Hot, dry desert,
   Sun beating down.
   A man seen walking,
   Far from the town.

   CHORUS
   (*mf*) "I need water – quickly! I pray,
   Oh, God, please guide me, show me the way."

2. (*f*) A well of water!
   Man runs to see
   (*mf*) No bucket hangs there,
   How can this be?

   CHORUS
   (*p*) "Sock my vessel, rope is my aid,
   I'm slipping, sliding, feel quite afraid."

3. (*mf*) Water gathered,
   Losing no time.
   (*mp*) Feels weary, out now,
   Worn with the climb.

   CHORUS
   (*mf*) "Thank you, God, but what do I see?
   A thirsty, dying dog close to me."

4. (*mp*) Full of care
   He stops not to think.
   (*mf*) He gives the dog
   The life-saving drink.

   CHORUS
   (*f*) "I need water – quickly! I pray."
   And God was pleased and showed him the way.
   Amen.

**SHEET 1**

**A WORLD OF LIGHT** · SCHOFIELD & SIMS LTD

# The Lama and the Fish

**UNIT 7**
**A story for assembly based on the Buddhist faith**

Sengge, the King's son, Trisong, son of one of the King's ministers, and Rabsel, a merchant's son, were playing by the river one day, throwing stones into the water. A large fish swam into view and the boys tried to stone it. They could not manage to harm the fish and began to argue with each other about where the life of a fish lay. Sengge was convinced that life lay in the head of a fish, Trisong that the fish's life lay in its stomach and Rabsel thought that the fish's tail contained its life. An argument, followed by a fight was the result and as they fought the fish swam away.

Each boy wished to be proved right and the tutor, who separated the boys and stopped the fight, suggested they went to ask the Lama, who lived in the monastery nearby.

One day of each week was a feast day, when the people of the city visited the monastery, made offerings to their god, and made requests to the Lama. The boys decided to go together to ask the Lama to settle the problem.

The boys could not wait for the feast day, and none of them could risk the Lama proving him wrong. Therefore each one took a gift to the Lama before the feast day, to ensure that he would receive the answer he wanted. Sengge took a gold coin, Trisong his beautiful new sword and Rabsel some fresh meat. In each case, the Lama agreed to give the answer required.

On the day of the feast the three boys appeared before the Lama and told him the cause of their argument, as if they had not been to him before. The Lama told them that they were all correct, that there were three kinds of fish: those who had life in their heads, those who had life in their stomachs and those who had it in their tails. The boys were well satisfied with the Lama's words and went away happily, the best of friends again!

The Lama had three good presents: a gold coin, a beautiful sword and enough meat to last him many days!

**A WORLD OF LIGHT · SCHOFIELD & SIMS LTD**

**SHEET 1**

## UNIT 7
### A play for assembly based on the Buddhist faith

# The Lama and the Fish

**CHARACTERS**
Prince Sengge of Ladakh, a boy of about twelve
Trisong, a minister's son
Rabsel, a merchant's son
The Lama
Seeva, the Lama's servant
Garpa, Prince Sengge's tutor
Sengge's servant

## Scene One

*In the village of Ladakh, in the Himalayan mountains. Sengge, Trisong and Rabsel, the three boys, are playing on the bank of the river and throwing stones into the water. Garpa sits nearby.*

**RABSEL** *excitedly*

Look, our stones have disturbed that large fish.

**SENGGE**

It's huge. Quick! Hit it! Hit it on the head!

*He flings a stone at the fish.*

**TRISONG** *jeering*

Missed! You could have hit its body but you aimed for its head. Why?

**SENGGE**

Because that's where its life is, in its head. That's why.

*He picks up another stone.*

**TRISONG**

Don't be stupid. A fish's life is in its stomach. My mother says so.

**SENGGE** *scornfully*

You're the one who is stupid. Everyone knows a fish's life is in its head.

**RABSEL** *quietly*

My grandfather is the oldest man in the city, and he says a fish's life is in its tail. If we want to kill the fish, we should aim at its tail.

**TRISONG** *pushing him*

You don't know what you're talking about. You are even more stupid than Sengge.

**SENGGE** *angrily*

And you are the most stupid of all.

*He hits Trisong who hits him back and the two boys start to fight. Rabsel joins in against Trisong, and the three boys are*

SHEET 1

# The Lama and the Fish

*finally separated by Sengge's tutor, who pulls them apart.*

**GARPA** *shocked*

Your Highness, what are you thinking of? You are rolling about like a common street boy. And you two, your fathers will hear something today when I tell them.

**SENGGE** *crossly*

Oh, be quiet, Garpa. Mind your own business.

**RABSEL**

The fish has gone.

*The three boys rush to the river's edge and then start to laugh.*

**SENGGE**

It swam away as we were fighting.

**GARPA** *exasperated*

What are you laughing about?

**RABSEL** *gasping*

It's about the fish. We were fighting because we couldn't agree where a fish's life is. We've all got different ideas.

**SENGGE** *soberly*

Do you know where the life of a fish is to be found, Garpa? I think it's in its head, Rabsel says it's in its tail and Trisong thinks it's in its stomach.

**GARPA**

I don't know where the life of a fish is, but if you are so keen to know, why don't you ask the person who knows everything – the Lama himself.

**SENGGE**

Yes, that's an idea. We'll see him on the feast day this week.

*He turns to the others.*

Shall we do that then? The Lama will tell us the truth.

**RABSEL** *nodding*

Yes, I agree to that. What about you, Trisong?

**TRISONG**

Yes, let's forget it now. I want to show you all my new sword. I got it for my birthday from my Uncle Chovul.

**SENGGE** *surprised*

You never told us. Why not?

---

57  A WORLD OF LIGHT · SCHOFIELD & SIMS LTD

SHEET 2

# The Lama and the Fish

**TRISONG**

I only got it at the weekend. I was going to surprise you. Come on to my house.

*The three boys hurry away, arm in arm, leaving Garpa.*

**GARPA** *sighing*

One minute they're fighting, the next they're the best of friends. Oh, well, they're just children after all.

**SEEVA** *approaching*

Talking to yourself, Garpa? What have these young imps been up to?

**GARPA** *laughing*

Fighting over where a fish's life is to be found. They're going to ask his Holiness, so you'd better warn him. Whoever wins the argument will make life unbearable for the other two.

**SEEVA**

I'll warn him. They'll be coming with presents I shouldn't wonder. His Holiness will think of something. He always does.

**GARPA**

I'd better follow those young rascals. They've gone to young Trisong's house and he and the Prince haven't done any studying today.

*He moves away as the scene ends.*

## Scene Two

*Inside the Lama's monastery the following evening. A bell is heard chiming. In the almost bare room the Lama is sitting on a throne (back centre). Seeva enters, folds his hands and bows to the Lama.*

**LAMA** *quietly*

What is it, Seeva? It isn't the day for visitors and yet I'm aware there are some here.

**SEEVA**

Holiness, it's Prince Sengge and his two friends, though none knows the others are here. I've put them in separate rooms.

**LAMA** *amused*

That was a good idea. It would not be wise to see them together at this point. Each one is determined to gain my support, I suppose. You had better send one of them in, whichever one arrived first.

# The Lama and the Fish

**SEEVA**

Yes, Holiness.

*He bows and hurries out. A few moments later, Sengge enters, followed by a servant. Both bow to Lama.*

**LAMA** *quietly*

Did you offer a prayer to God Manjish before you came in here?

**SENGGE** *eagerly*

Yes, Holiness.

*He turns to his servant.*

Give the Lama the gold coin.

*The servant lays a gold coin at Lama's feet, bows and stands back.*

**LAMA**

Speak on, Prince Sengge. What is your request? It isn't the usual day for it, you know.

**SENGGE** *humbly*

I know, Holiness, but my friends and I have had an argument. It led to a fight.

**LAMA** *gravely*

I am sorry to hear that. Fighting never solves problems, Prince Sengge.

**SENGGE**

I know. We are friends again now. It was about a fish, you see. We can't decide where its life is. I think it is in the head of a fish but Trisong thinks it is in its stomach, and Rabsel thinks it is in its tail. It couldn't be in its stomach or its tail, at least, I don't think so. Will you please say on the feast night, when we all come together, that it is in its head?

**LAMA** *smiling*

Very well, Prince Sengge. I shall say that the life of a fish is in its head.

**SENGGE** *gratefully*

Oh, thank you, your Holiness.

*He bows low.*

I will see you on the feast night.

*He backs out of the room, followed by his servant, who does the same.*

**SEEVA** *entering after a long pause*

Trisong, Holiness. He wishes to speak with you.

**TRISONG** *entering and bowing to the Lama*

Holiness, I have a request to make, but first, I would like to offer my sword as a gift.

*He unbuckles his beautiful sword and lays it at the Lama's feet.*

**LAMA**

Thank you, Trisong. How can I help you? Have you made your prayer?

SHEET 4

# The Lama and the Fish

**TRISONG**

Yes, my friends and I have had an argument. It led to a fight...

**LAMA** *sadly*

How unfortunate. Fights do not solve anything, my son.

**TRISONG** *sadly*

I know, Holiness. You see, my friends and I were arguing about a fish. Sengge says that a fish's life is in its head and Rabsel that it is in its tail. Yet I know that the life of a fish is in its stomach because my mother says so.

**LAMA** *quietly*

I see.

**TRISONG**

So I wondered if, when we come to see you at the feast on Wednesday, you would say that the life of a fish is in its stomach, please.

**LAMA**

Yes, of course I will.

**TRISONG** *gratefully*

Oh, thank you, Holiness.

*He bows to the Lama and backs out of the room.*

**SEEVA** *entering*

Holiness, young Rabsel is here to see you. I kept him back until Trisong had gone. He was most anxious that neither Trisong nor Prince Sengge should know that he came to see you.

**LAMA** *smiling*

Send him in, please.

**RABSEL** *entering and bowing to the Lama*

Good evening, Holiness.

**LAMA** *pleasantly*

Good evening, Rabsel. How are you?

**RABSEL**

I am well, thank you, Holiness, but I have a problem.

**LAMA**

I am sorry to hear that, Rabsel. Tell me about it.

**RABSEL**

First, I would like to give you this, Holiness.

# The Lama and the Fish

*He produces some fresh meat, wrapped in a skin.*

It is fresh meat, Holiness. Father bought it and I paid him out of my own money.

**LAMA** *pleased*

Thank you, Rabsel.

**RABSEL**

You see, Holiness, my friends and I have been quarrelling and fighting.

**LAMA** *sadly*

Oh, dear. I'm sorry to hear that, Rabsel. It isn't like you to fight.

**RABSEL**

I know, Holiness, but you see, it was about the fish. We saw a fish, and Sengge said that a fish's life was in its head but I know it's in its tail. My grandfather said so, and he is a wise man.

**LAMA**

Indeed he is, Rabsel and I haven't seen him for some time. Is he well?

**RABSEL**

Yes, thank you, Holiness, but about the fish . . .

**LAMA** *hastily*

Oh, yes. What do you want me to do?

**RABSEL**

On the Feast Day we'll all be coming to see you. Will you say that a fish's life is in its tail, please?

**LAMA** *warmly*

Of course I will, Rabsel. You can rely on me.

**RABSEL** *delighted*

Oh, thank you, Lama.

*He bows and backs out of the room.*

# The Lama and the Fish

## Scene Three

*Two days later. Sengge, Trisong and Rabsel reach the monastery, dressed in their best clothes. They bow before the god at the shrine (far right) and make their way to the Lama, who is sitting in his chair (far left).*

**BOYS** *bowing*

Good evening, Holiness.

**LAMA** *pleasantly*

Good evening, boys. You are all looking smart, I see. What can I do for you?

**SENGGE** *bowing again*

Truth is like gold, is it not Holiness?

**LAMA**

Yes, indeed it is, Sengge.

**RABSEL**

Truth is like fresh meat wrapped in a skin, Holiness, isn't it?

**LAMA**

Yes, indeed, Rabsel.

**TRISONG** *bowing*

When one has a problem, the truth of it is as the cut of a sword, isn't it, Holiness?

**LAMA**

Yes, it is, Trisong, but where is all this leading? What do you all want?

**SENGGE**

I will explain, Holiness. You see, my friends and I have had an argument and we wish to know the truth of the matter. It is about the life of a fish.

**LAMA**

Indeed?

**SENGGE**

I think that a fish's life is in its head, but the others disagree.

**TRISONG**

I believe a fish has life in its stomach, Holiness.

**RABSEL**

I think the life of a fish is in its tail, Holiness.

**SENGGE**

So we came to you, Holiness. Can you please tell us which of us is right?

# The Lama and the Fish

**LAMA**

You all are.

**BOYS** *amazed*

All of us?

**LAMA**

Yes. You see, there are three kinds of fish. One has life in its head, another has life in its stomach and the third has life in its tail. You are all right.

**BOYS** *pleased*

Thank you, Lama.

*Sengge, Trisong and Rabsel bow to the Lama and make their way out right.*

**LAMA**

And I am happy too. I have three beautiful presents and look forward to eating my meat tonight!

*He turns to greet his next visitors with a smile, as the play ends.*

SHEET 8

# UNIT 7
**A song for assembly based on the Buddhist faith**

# The Lama and the Fish

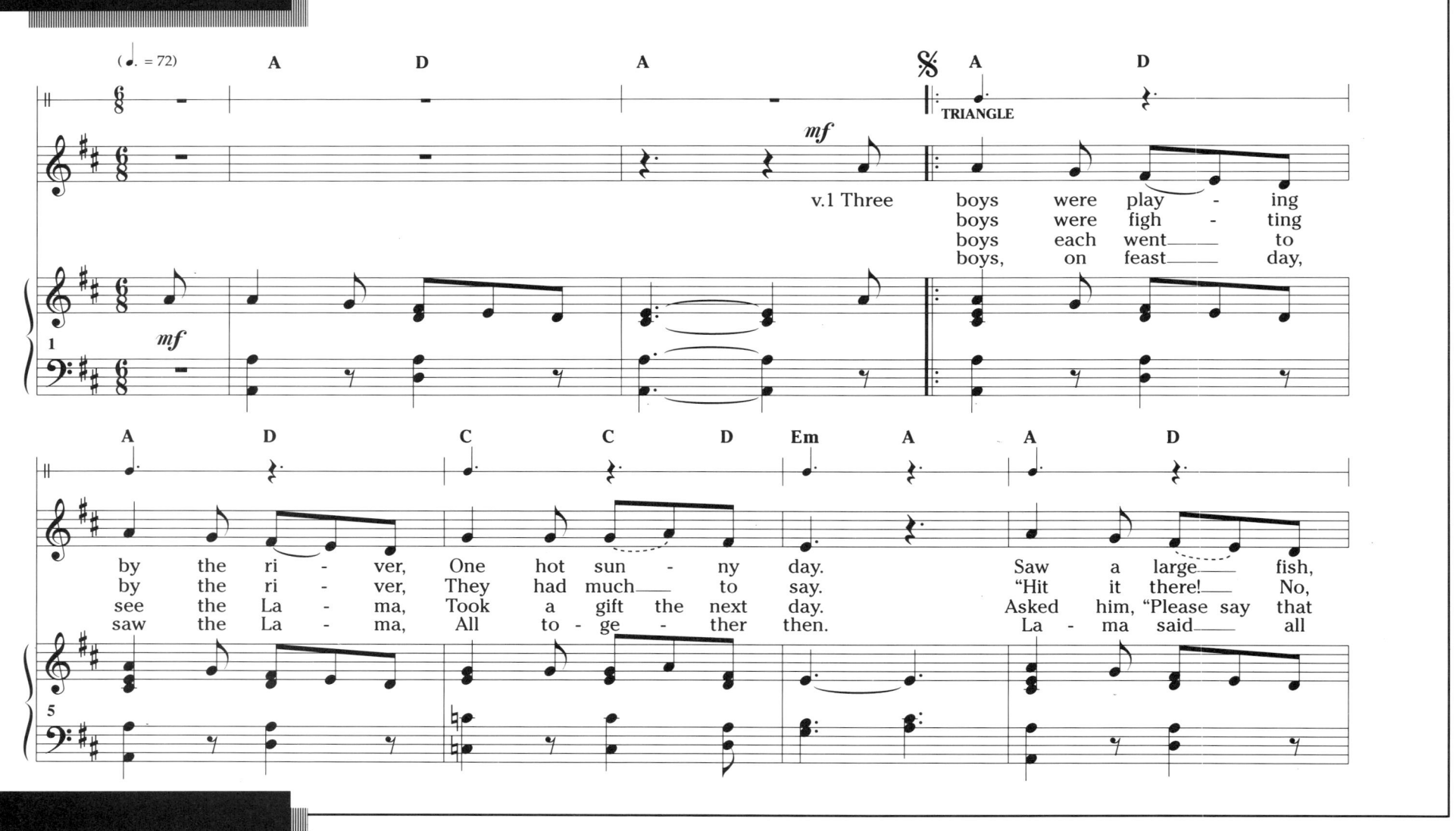

(♩. = 72)

v.1 Three boys were play-ing by the ri-ver, One hot sun-ny day. Saw a large fish, "Hit it there! No,
    boys were figh-ting by the ri-ver, They had much to say. Asked him, "Please say that
    boys each went to see the La-ma, Took a gift the next day. La-ma said all
    boys, on feast day, saw the La-ma, All to-ge-ther then.

SHEET 1

A WORLD OF LIGHT · SCHOFIELD & SIMS LTD   64

# The Lama and the Fish

*(lyrics under music)*

vv.1&3:
tried to catch\_\_\_ it, Each one thought he knew the right way. v.2 Three
that's not right!"\_\_\_ Fish flicked its tail, swam
I am right,"\_\_\_ The La - ma said, "I will. Now a - way!" v.4 Three
three were right,\_\_\_ They went a - way best

vv.2&4:
swift - ly a - way. Where does the life of a fish lie? In its
friends once a - gain. Where does the life of a fish lie? In its

65  A WORLD OF LIGHT · SCHOFIELD & SIMS LTD

SHEET 2

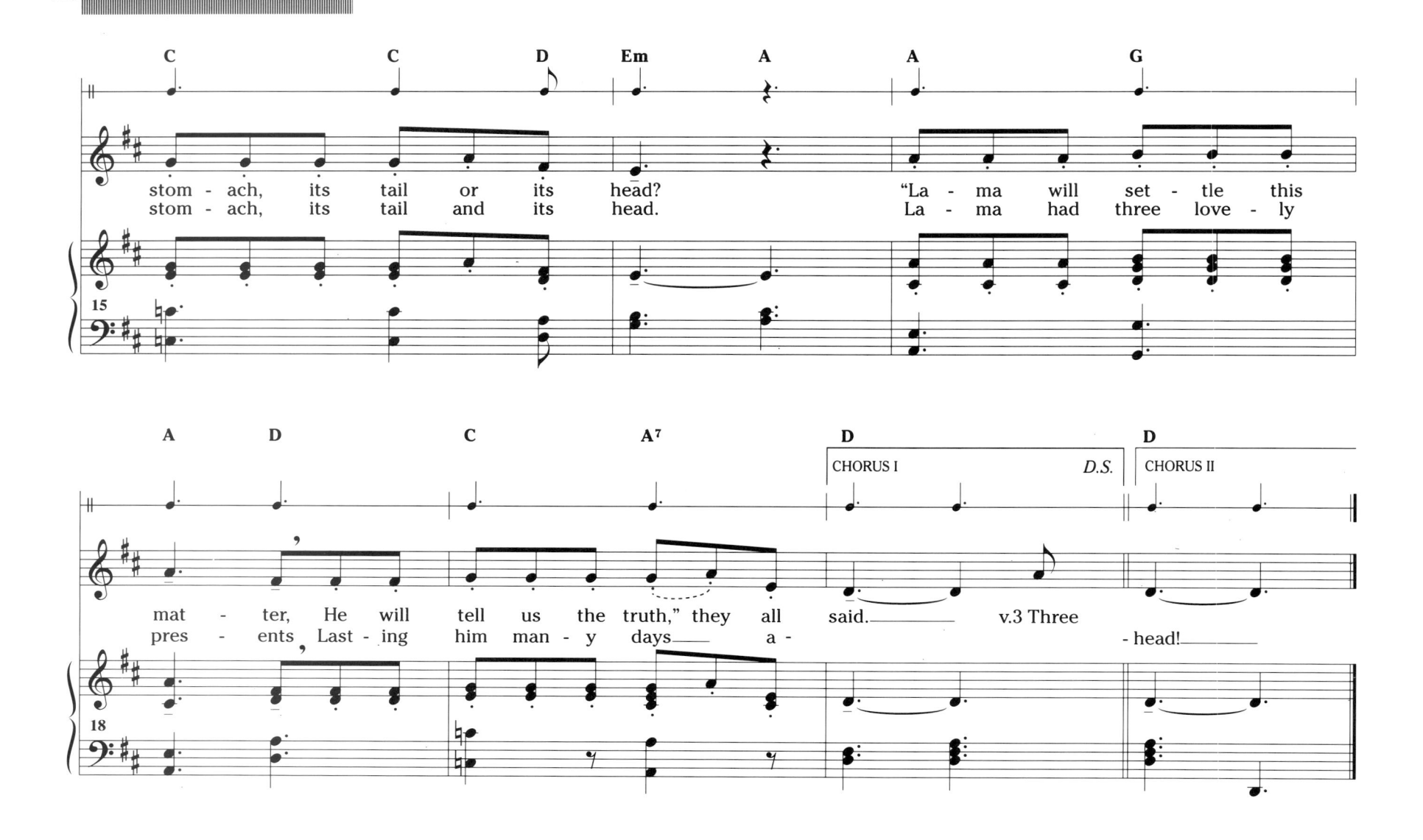

# The Lama and the Fish

stom - ach, its tail or its head? "La - ma will set - tle this
stom - ach, its tail and its head. La - ma had three love - ly
mat - ter, He will tell us the truth," they all said. v.3 Three
pres - ents, Last - ing him man - y days a - - head!

CHORUS I  D.S.  CHORUS II

SHEET 3

A WORLD OF LIGHT · SCHOFIELD & SIMS LTD  66

# The Lama and the Fish

**UNIT 7**
**A song for assembly based on the Buddhist faith**

1. *(mf)* Three boys were playing by the river,
   One hot sunny day.
   Saw a large fish, tried to catch it,
   Each one thought he knew the right way.

2. *(f)* Three boys were fighting by the river,
   They had much to say.
   "Hit it there! No, that's not right!"
   Fish flicked its tail, swam swiftly away.

   CHORUS I
   *(mf)* Where does the life of a fish lie?
   In its stomach, its tail or its head?
   "Lama will settle this matter,
   He will tell us the truth," they all said.

3. *(mf)* Three boys each went to see the Lama,
   Took a gift the next day.
   Asked him, "Please say that I am right,"
   The Lama said, "I will. Now away!"

4. *(mf)* Three boys, on feast day, saw the Lama,
   All together then.
   Lama said all three were right,
   They went away best friends once again.

   *(f)* CHORUS II
   Where does the life of a fish lie?
   In its stomach, its tail and its head.
   Lama had three lovely presents
   Lasting him many days ahead!

**A WORLD OF LIGHT** · SCHOFIELD & SIMS LTD

SHEET 1

## UNIT 8
**A play for assembly based on the Jewish faith**

# Ruth and Naomi – A Story of Friendship

### CHARACTERS
Naomi, a widow from Bethlehem
Orpah }
Ruth } Naomi's daughters-in-law
Boaz, a wealthy farmer
Overseer
Hannah, a worker in the field
Miriam, Naomi's relative
Young Men
Reapers
Gleaners

## Scene One

*In Naomi's house, in Moab, Orpah and Ruth are talking together.*

**ORPAH** *anxiously*

What do you think will happen to us all, Ruth? Naomi hasn't said anything for days and we're running out of food.

**RUTH** *comfortingly*

I'm sure Naomi will think of something. It's been much harder for her than it has been for us.

**ORPAH** *shocked*

How can it be harder for Naomi? We've lost our husbands and we're only young.

**RUTH**

Our husbands were Naomi's sons. Don't forget that. She's struggled all these years to bring them up and for what? Now she's got us on her hands and she's not even from these parts.

**NAOMI** *entering and holding out her hands to the girls*

Ah, there you are, my daughters. Come and sit down so that we can make our plans.

*They sit beside her on either side of the table*

**RUTH** *eagerly*

You've decided something, Mother?

**NAOMI** *gently*

I like it when you call me 'Mother' because you two are like real daughters to me. You know that, don't you?

**ORPAH** *nodding*

Yes, Mother.

SHEET 1

A WORLD OF LIGHT · SCHOFIELD & SIMS LTD   68

# Ruth and Naomi

**NAOMI** *holding their hands*

And I want you to know that you will always be special to me, even when we are apart.

**RUTH** *fearfully*

Apart? You're...you're going away, Mother?

**NAOMI**

In Bethlehem, where I come from, it will soon be harvest time. There will be food to spare for a widow like me...my nephew is a farmer and he will look after me.

**RUTH**

But what about us? What will we do?

**NAOMI** *quietly*

You and Orpah have families here in Moab. You can go back to them and they will take care of you.

**ORPAH** *doubtfully*

Go home? Oh, I don't know...

**NAOMI**

You've kept in touch with your family. They love you, don't they?

**ORPAH**

Yes, yes, of course, but...

**NAOMI** *firmly*

Then they will look after you. Your parents will be pleased to have you back. You are both young. You will marry again, both of you.

**RUTH**

You might marry again.

**NAOMI** *amazed*

Me? Oh, I don't think so. I'm too old.

**RUTH**

You told us that in Bethlehem when a woman loses her husband, the oldest unmarried man in your family marries the widow.

**NAOMI**

Even so, I've no wish to marry again, but I do need the help of my relatives and I will be all right. Now, the sooner we start to prepare for our journeys the better. Why don't you two begin to pack your belongings and tomorrow I'll send messages to your families to expect you home soon.

**ORPAH** *doubtfully*

If you're sure...

SHEET 2

# Ruth and Naomi

**NAOMI** *firmly*

I am. It will be for the best, you'll see.

**ORPAH**

I'll go and sort my clothes out then.

*She goes out.*

**NAOMI**

Ruth, won't you go with Orpah?

**RUTH** *quietly*

I'm staying.

**NAOMI** *surprised*

Staying? But I'm going back to Bethlehem, I thought you understood that.

**RUTH**

Yes, I do.

**NAOMI**

But there'll be no one here...

**RUTH**

When I said I was staying, I meant staying with you.

**NAOMI** *puzzled*

But how can you?

**RUTH** *calmly*

I'm going with you. I've made up my mind.

**NAOMI**

But, Ruth, your place is with your own people. Why should you want to come with me to a strange place?

**RUTH** *desperately*

Please, Naomi, don't tell me to leave you. Don't send me back. I want to be with you. You've been like a real mother to me and more than that, a true friend.

**NAOMI** *softly*

It's good to hear you say that, Ruth, but don't you see how hard it will be for you? We'll both be expected to work for our living in Bethlehem. We worship a different God, as you know, and I've no idea where I shall be living...

**RUTH** *firmly*

Mother Naomi, wherever you go, I shall go. Wherever you live, I shall live. Your people will be my people and your God my God.

SHEET 3

# Ruth and Naomi

**NAOMI** *hugging her*

Ruth, there is nothing I'd like better than to have you with me, but I had to be sure that you knew what we might have to face when we get there. Let's find Orpah and tell her that we will go back to her village with her tomorrow. Then we can see your parents at the same time and tell them that you will be leaving with me soon.

*Naomi and Ruth go out arm in arm.*

## Scene Two

*In Bethlehem, on the edge of large fields where groups of people are gathering corn and young girls are picking up anything the corn gatherers drop. A tall man, clearly in charge of the reapers and gleaners is giving directions.*

**OVERSEER**

Hurry now, everyone. Time is money, you know. I can see plenty of corn waiting to be picked up over there.

**RUTH** *timidly*

Excuse me.

**OVERSEER**

Yes? What is it?

**RUTH** *nervously*

Do you think I could work here, please?

**OVERSEER** *to the workers*

Keep in your own area. Boaz will be here soon, and he'll want to see the job well done.

*To Ruth*

You're new to these parts, aren't you?

**RUTH**

Yes, I'm from Moab. I came here yesterday with my mother-in-law.

**OVERSEER**

Oh, yes, I heard. You are the girl from Moab who wouldn't let Naomi travel by herself.

**RUTH**

Well . . . I wanted to be with her.

**OVERSEER** *kindly*

It's hard work, you know. But it's worth it.

# Ruth and Naomi

**RUTH**

What do I have to do?

**OVERSEER**

You have to follow closely behind the reapers — the men gathering in the corn — and pick up anything they drop. Most of it will be chaff, waste that isn't needed, but if you are lucky you'll find enough corn has been dropped for you to have enough to live on. I'll start you with young Hannah's group. They'll look after you, but you will have to move quickly because all the girls are like you, they need to collect as much as they can. Come over here.

*The Overseer leads Ruth to the far corner of the field and places her with a small group of girls her own age.*

**OVERSEER**

Hannah, here's a new girl. Show her how to glean, will you?

**HANNAH** *stopping work*

Why me? You know there's little enough for us on Jacob's patch.

**OVERSEER** *sharply*

It's only for today. I'll set her on somewhere else for tomorrow. I'll be back later to see how she's getting on.

*He strides away.*

**HANNAH** *not looking up*

Come on, then. Take your shawl in one hand and pick up the corn with the other. Hurry.

**RUTH** *panting*

Like this?

**HANNAH**

That's it, but you have to work up speed. Jacob keeps a close eye on his reapers to see they don't drop much and a lot of it is useless anyway. How come you've never done this before?

**RUTH** *breathlessly*

I've just got here from Moab.

**HANNAH** *stopping suddenly*

Oh, you are Ruth, the Moabite woman.

**RUTH**

Yes. Why?

**HANNAH** *resuming work*

It's all over the town. You could have had an easy life but you chose to come here instead.

**REAPER**

Hey, new girl. You can work with me if you like.

**HANNAH**

Take no notice. The young men are always like that. Oh, look, Boaz has arrived.

SHEET 5

# Ruth and Naomi

**RUTH** *looking up*

Who?

**HANNAH**

Keep your eyes down. Boaz is rich. He owns half this field. Look at the overseer running round him.

**BOAZ** *loudly*

The Lord be with you.

**REAPERS**

May the Lord bless you, Boaz.

**RUTH**

Everyone seems to like him.

**HANNAH** *shortly*

Oh, yes. He's all right.

**BOAZ**

Overseer, have you taken on some new workers today?

**OVERSEER**

Yes, a few. Why, sir?

**BOAZ**

That young woman over at the far side, who is she?

**OVERSEER**

Oh, that's the Moabite girl. She needed work desperately to help Naomi, your relation.

**BOAZ**

Oh, of course. I heard Naomi had arrived. Tell the girl to come to see me, Overseer, please.

**OVERSEER**

Yes, sir.

*He hurries away to Ruth.*

Boaz wants you so you must come at once and be quick about it.

**RUTH** *nervously*

What...what does he want?

**OVERSEER** *sharply*

How should I know? Boaz gives the orders and I obey them. Come on, over to the middle of the field.

**HANNAH**

Take your corn with you. It isn't safe to leave it.

*Ruth hurries after the Overseer.*

A WORLD OF LIGHT · SCHOFIELD & SIMS LTD

SHEET **6**

# Ruth and Naomi

**OVERSEER** *pleasantly*

This is the girl, sir.

**BOAZ** *kindly*

Well, have you managed to gather much today? Let me see.

**RUTH** *opening her shawl*

Not much, I'm afraid.

**BOAZ**

You can join the gleaners in my part of the field and I'll tell the reapers to drop as much corn as they can for you.

**RUTH** *amazed*

That's very kind of you sir, but why?

**BOAZ**

You could have gone back to your family in Moab and might never have had to work, yet you chose to come here with Naomi and work to help her and support yourself. That was a brave and loyal thing to do. We must help you all we can. In future you will work on my land only. Have you had a drink of water since you started work today?

**OVERSEER** *interrupting*

After a late arrival this morning, she has worked without any break at all, sir.

**BOAZ**

Go and tell my servants to give you a drink from my pitcher. From now on, you will have enough food to keep you and Naomi for ever.

*As Ruth tries to kneel before him he waves her away.*

## Scene Three

*Early evening in Naomi's small cottage. Naomi is watching anxiously for Ruth's arrival.*

**RUTH** *reaching the door*

Here I am at last, Mother Naomi.

**NAOMI** *warmly*

Oh, Ruth, you must be tired. You are not used to the work — what's this? Ruth, you can't have gathered all this corn in one day.

**RUTH** *cheerfully*

No, but Boaz added to it. He says he will make sure we have enough food forever.

**NAOMI** *delighted*

Oh, I can't believe it. Ruth, it's a miracle. How did you manage it?

SHEET 7

A WORLD OF LIGHT · SCHOFIELD & SIMS LTD   74

# Ruth and Naomi

**RUTH** *laughing*

I didn't do anything. Boaz just sent for me and told me I'd be working for him in future and he told the reapers to drop as much corn as they could for me.

**NAOMI** *thoughtfully*

Boaz is not our oldest unmarried relative. Zebulun is our oldest unmarried relative.

**RUTH** *sitting down at the table*

What do you mean, Mother?

**NAOMI**

Oh, nothing...well, Boaz isn't married, you know, and you need to have a husband. It's our rule that if any of our women are widowed the oldest unmarried relative marries her.

**RUTH**

But I'm not one of your people.

**NAOMI** *crossly*

Of course you are. You said yourself, "Your people will be my people and your God my God." It works both ways, Ruth. You chose to join my people and will be treated as one. Now come along, have your meal. Your Aunt Miriam said she'd call tonight and she'll be here any minute.

**MIRIAM** *entering*

Naomi?

**NAOMI** *warmly*

Yes, come in, Miriam.

**MIRIAM** *excitedly*

Hello, Ruth. Naomi, such goings on. You'd never believe it.

**NAOMI**

What goings on, Miriam?

**MIRIAM**

As soon as work was over, Boaz went to the town to go to see the elders. He is talking now with them and they've sent for Zebulun.

**NAOMI** *startled*

For Zebulun? Is it about Ruth?

**MIRIAM**

Yes, I'm certain it is. Boaz told his cousins he was going to ask Zebulun about his duty...about marrying Ruth.

**NAOMI** *disappointed*

Oh, I see.

A WORLD OF LIGHT · SCHOFIELD & SIMS LTD

SHEET 8

# Ruth and Naomi

**RUTH**

But I don't want to marry anyone. I've only just arrived.

**NAOMI** *unhappily*

Unfortunately, it's our law, Ruth. I just didn't think it would happen so quickly.

**RUTH**

And what is Zebulun like?

**MIRIAM** *carefully*

Oh, he's . . . well, he's . . . he's getting on in years. He'll look after you well, I'm sure.

**NAOMI**

But why did Boaz take it upon himself to ask Zebulun to marry Ruth?

**MIRIAM**

I don't know, but Sarah, she's Boaz's cousin, she said she'd let me know if she heard anything.

**NAOMI** *sadly*

Oh, well, I expect we'll hear soon enough. Oh . . . was that a knock I heard?

**MIRIAM**

Yes, I'm sure it was.

*Naomi goes to the door.*

**MIRIAM** *kindly*

You look worn out, Ruth. Why don't you go to bed?

**NAOMI** *entering*

Ruth, I have some surprising news. There is a young man outside, with a message from Boaz.

**RUTH** *astonished*

From Boaz? At this time of night?

**MIRIAM**

Never mind what time it is. Go and see the young man.

*As Ruth goes out the two women smile at each other.*

**MIRIAM**

Well? It can't be that Zebulun wants to marry Ruth or you wouldn't be smiling like this.

**RUTH** *entering*

I . . . I can't believe it.

**MIRIAM** *impatiently*

Believe what?

SHEET 9

A WORLD OF LIGHT · SCHOFIELD & SIMS LTD   76

# Ruth and Naomi

**RUTH**

Boaz sent his servant to ask if we — you and I, mother — will go to his house tomorrow one hour after sunrise to discuss whether or not I'll be prepared to marry him. It seems that Zebulun doesn't want to be married but Boaz does. He wants to marry me.

**MIRIAM** *excitedly*

Well, who would have thought it? Boaz, himself.

**NAOMI**

I think we must ask Ruth what she feels about this.

**RUTH**

I hadn't thought about your law, that widows must marry, but Boaz is a kind man and I like him.

**NAOMI** *briskly*

Well, that's a good start anyway. Now, off to bed, young lady. We're to be up early tomorrow.

★ ★ ★

Ruth and Boaz did marry and had a happy life together. Their son, Obed, was the great-grandfather of David, the great Jewish king.

# From Naomi To Ruth

**UNIT 8**
*A song for assembly based on the Jewish faith*

**SHEET 1**

Lyrics:
My faith-ful friend, How can I thank you? Your car-ing ways and your

A WORLD OF LIGHT · SCHOFIELD & SIMS LTD    78

G Am Am Em Dm Am Em
thought - ful - ness. The one I trust, The one who
11
F C Am Em Dm G Am
to Coda
loves me. In know - ing you I am rich - ly blessed.
16

# From Naomi to Ruth

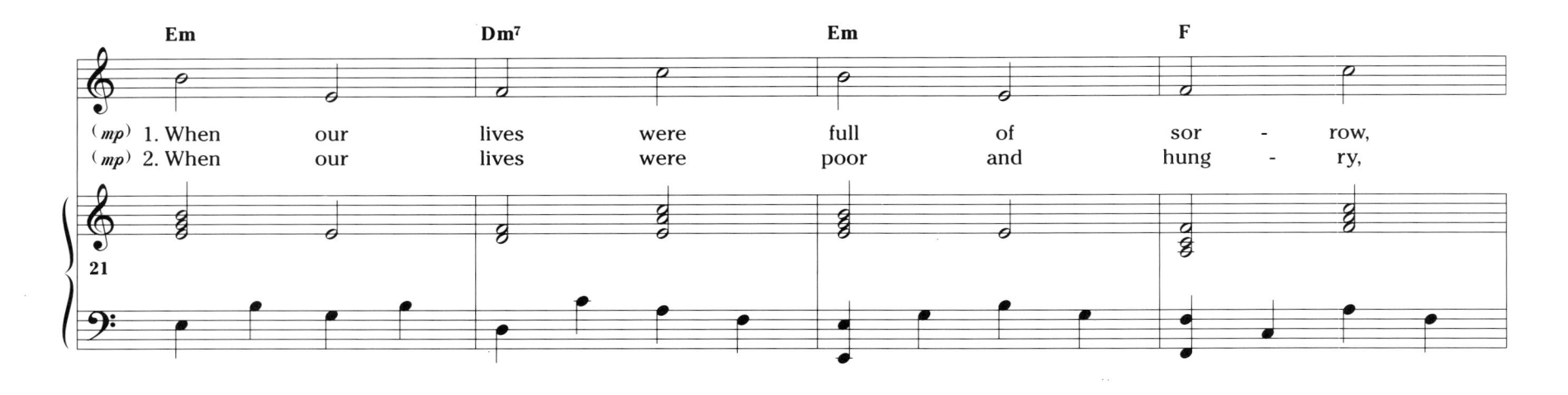

1. When our lives were full of sor-row,
2. When our lives were poor and hung-ry,

You took me by the hand.
You gath-ered in the grain.

SHEET 3

# From Naomi to Ruth

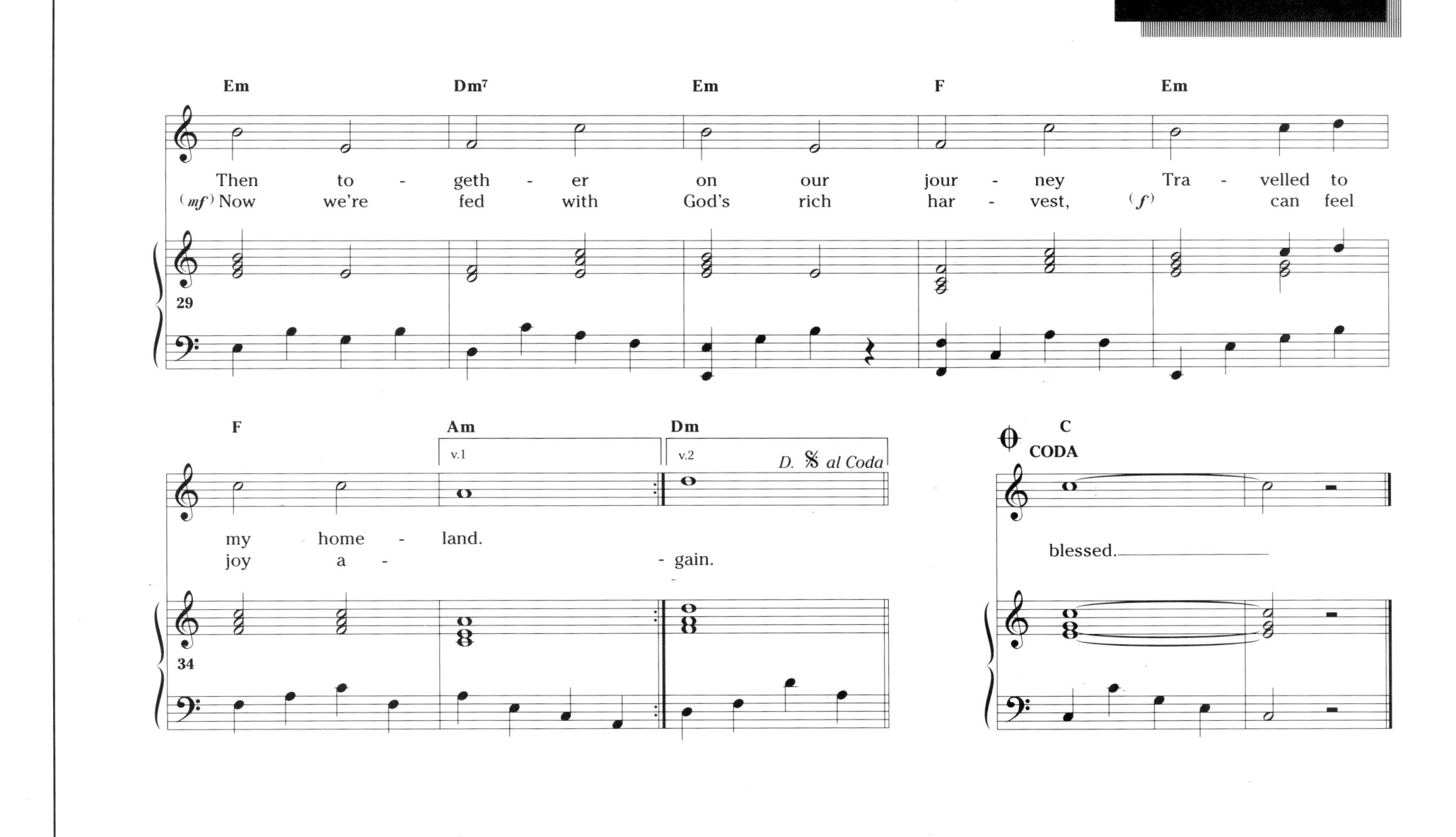

Then to-geth-er on our jour-ney, Tra-velled to
(mf) Now we're fed with God's rich har-vest, (f) can feel

my home-land.
joy a - gain.

blessed.

81  A WORLD OF LIGHT · SCHOFIELD & SIMS LTD

SHEET 4

**UNIT 8**

**A song for assembly based on the Jewish faith**

# From Naomi to Ruth

    (*mf*) CHORUS
        My faithful friend,
        How can I thank you?
        Your caring ways and your thoughtfulness.
        The one I trust,
        The one who loves me.
        In knowing you I am richly blessed.

1.   (*mp*) When our lives were full of sorrow,
        You took me by the hand.
        Then together on our journey
        Travelled to my homeland.

    CHORUS

2.   (*mp*) When our lives were poor and hungry
        You gathered in the grain.
    (*mf*) Now we're fed with God's rich harvest,
    (*f*) We can feel joy again.

    CHORUS

**SHEET 1**

**A WORLD OF LIGHT** · SCHOFIELD & SIMS LTD

# Kori's Dream

**UNIT 9
A story for assembly based on the Hindu faith**

Kori lived in a small village outside the large city of Calcutta at the beginning of this century. His father had a jewellery business in Calcutta and Kori's two older brothers were training to be jewellers like their father. When Kori left school he was to join his brothers in the shop.

Kori did not want to be a jeweller. He wanted to be an artist and almost every day his teachers shouted at him or called at his home to tell his parents that once again Kori was refusing to do any schoolwork.

"He never pays attention in class and he draws all over his school books," they said. "He'll never learn anything this way."

"Kori, if you do not listen to your teachers I will take all your chalks and pencils away from you," threatened his father. "How can you help with the family business if you don't know anything?"

"I don't want to help with the family business," replied Kori. "I want to be an artist. You know that."

"No son of mine will be an artist." His father took his chalks and broke them into little pieces. "You will work in my shop like your brothers."

"I won't," answered Kori and his father was angry. "I forbid you to draw ever again," he shouted.

It made no difference. Kori borrowed some chalks and went on drawing. He drew everything: birds, wild animals, flowers, fruit. He could not seem to stop.

"He's really very good at drawing," his mother told his father who would not listen.

When Kori was ten years old his father told him he would now leave school, since he still refused to do any work.

"You can start at the shop tomorrow," he said. "You'll have no time to waste on drawing then."

"Father, can't I go to the Temple and ask the Goddess Kali if I am to be an artist or a jeweller?" asked Kori. "If the Goddess says I am to be a jeweller I won't argue about it ever again."

"I think that's a good idea." His father was pleased. "You can come with me to one of the Calcutta temples."

"I'd like to go to the old temple in the country," replied Kori. "I can get a lift with the potter. He's going there to deliver some pots the day after tomorrow."

"I don't know about that," began his father doubtfully, but Kori pleaded so hard that his father finally gave way.

"Take enough food with you because you might not be able to get back the same night," he said. "And I expect an answer one way or the other when you get back."

Kori set off the next morning. He climbed into the potter's cart and he had eaten most of the food his mother had given him by the time they reached the tiny village where the ancient temple of Kali stood open to the sun and wind. It had four walls but no roof, and small animals, birds and flowers could be seen everywhere inside the temple.

Kori, clutching a box of chalks his friend the potter had given him, walked into the temple and found a corner at the back where he could say his prayers to the Goddess. The temple was crowded, mainly, by late morning, with women and elderly people, since most of the younger men were at work. Sometimes, some of the worshippers would go outside to sit in the courtyard behind the temple to eat their midday meal which they had brought with

**A WORLD OF LIGHT · SCHOFIELD & SIMS LTD**

**SHEET 1**

# Kori's Dream

them. Kori joined them and was given rice and boiled water by kindly visitors.

The huge statue of the Goddess Kali at the front of the temple was surrounded by garlands of flowers and when Kori went back to the temple he made his way to the shrine and spoke to the Goddess from his heart.

"Please, Holy Mother, show me whether or not it is your wish for me to be an artist," he prayed. "Your temple is full of flowers and the birds come in to sing for you. I can draw these on your temple walls and make them beautiful if you will let me be an artist. And of course I'll be a jeweller if you want me to be one," he added hastily to be fair to his father.

Other people were coming to the shrine and Kori returned to his place at the back of the temple. He was tired and his eyes began to close. When he awoke it was dark and the temple was empty. He struggled to his feet and ran to the heavy door but it was locked. Kori was afraid at first but when he saw the soft glow from the lamps by the shrine he was comforted.

"Kali will protect me," he thought and made his way back to his corner. How long he slept he would never know, but suddenly the temple door opened with a bang. A man rushed in but Kori could not see where he went until he saw him standing in front of the Goddess' shrine.

"I'd better get out quickly," Kori thought and crept towards the door.

"Please, Goddess," the man was saying loudly, "All I wanted to do was build you a lovely new temple. I'm the ruler here and I have the money to do it. Why won't the people listen to me? Why are they objecting to me pulling this temple down when they can have a brand new one in its place? Please, Goddess. The builders will be here tomorrow. Don't you want a new temple?"

Someone else came in. Kori saw a tall man go up to the man by the shrine but he did not listen to any more. He hurried through the open door and hid round the corner of the temple. A few minutes later he saw the two men leave the temple and climb into the rickshaw led by two fine horses.

When Kori woke again it was dawn and he wondered if he had dreamed it all. Had a man – a King – really come to the temple in the middle of the night and prayed to the Goddess? Was he really going to pull this beautiful old temple down and build a new one? Was there something he, Kori, could do?

"All I can do is to keep my promise to the Goddess and draw the birds, the flowers and the small animals who come into the temple with the people," he thought. He took his chalks and began to draw. On the walls of the temple, on the floor of the courtyard, beautiful drawings began to appear. Kori was so busy that he did not notice the worshippers coming to the temple, or the temple priests, but he did hear the shouts when the demolition men arrived. Crowds of angry people were standing at the entrance to the courtyard shouting at the men who had come to pull their temple down. "Go away," they cried. "We've told the ruler he can't do this."

The men did not know what to do, but then the ruler arrived with his ministers. "Out of the way, everyone," he ordered. "Let the men do their work."

Kori made his way through the crowd. He folded his hands and bowed his head politely to the King.

"Please, sir. The Goddess Kali does not want you to pull her temple down," he said.

The ruler looked down at the small boy.

"And how do you know that?" he asked.

"She told me," replied Kori. "She told me to draw all the birds and little creatures who come in with us to pray. Look, I have drawn them for you."

The King followed Kori through the angry crowd to the temple courtyard and stared in amazement at the birds and flowers Kori had drawn.

SHEET 2

# Kori's Dream

"You did this?" he asked. "When did you do it?"

"Last night I was locked in the temple and I heard you come in and ask the Goddess to tell you if she wanted a temple or not," Kori answered. "This morning I felt she wanted me to draw the little creatures and flowers because she likes them to be here and the people like to share the temple with them."

"But why were you in the temple?" asked the King. "Did you want the Goddess to give you an answer to something, too?"

"I want to be an artist," answered Kori. "My father says I must be a jeweller. I came to ask the Goddess to decide."

"I think she has done that for both of us," said the King. He walked over to the demolition men.

"I have changed my mind," he told them. "The old temple will stay as it is."

A cheer went up from the crowd. The king put a friendly hand on Kori's shoulder.

"I have been silly," he said. "I didn't listen to the Goddess. She was speaking to me through all these people here and now she has spoken to me through you."

"She hasn't answered me, though," Kori said sadly.

"I think she has," replied the King. "You have saved her temple. You are a true artist with a great gift. You will come back home with me now and when you have eaten and rested we will visit your father."

Kori rode through the still excited crowd with the King. The ministers followed behind in their rickshaws. He was taken to the magnificent palace a few miles away and given breakfast and a bed where he could sleep.

Later that day there was great excitement in Kori's village when a horse-driven rickshaw stopped outside the little boy's house. Kori's father and mother and his two brothers came running out and they stared and stared as the King, richly dressed, was helped from his rickshaw by a proud Kori.

"What has he done?" asked Kori's father sternly, when he and his family had greeted the King.

"He has saved the Goddess's temple," answered the King. "And I have come to ask if he might come back with me to the palace and be trained as a court artist under some of the greatest painters in our land. He has a great gift."

For the first time, Kori's father was proud of his son and he agreed that Kali had given them all an answer to prayer.

Kori returned to the palace and trained under the guidance of great Indian artists. He became one of the best known artists of the century and is still living not far from the big city of Calcutta, a grandfather now, who loves to tell his grandchildren of the answer he had received from the Goddess Kali and which, at the time, he had thought to be a dream.

**UNIT 9**

# A song for assembly based on the Hindu faith

# Kori's Song

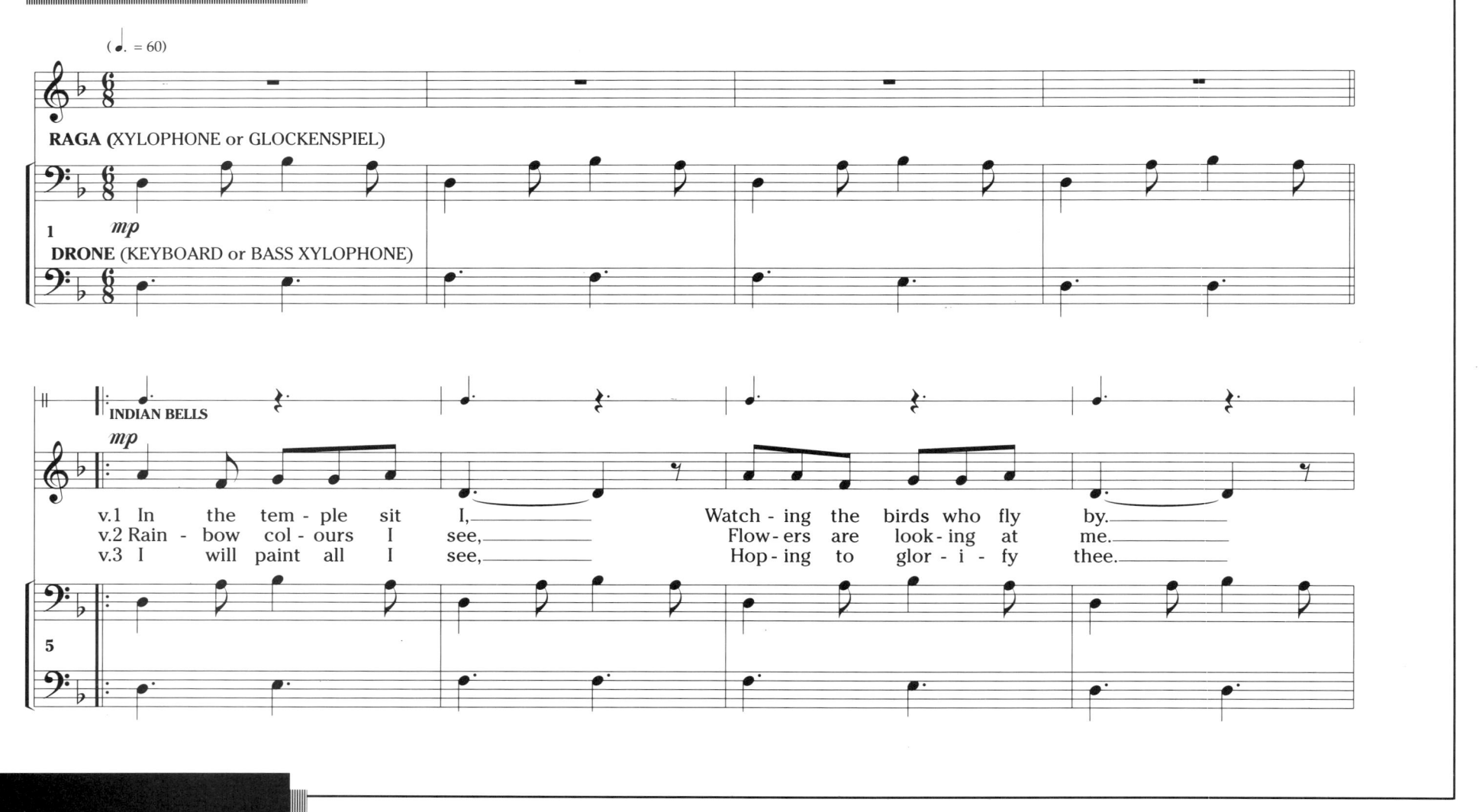

($\quad\bullet. = 60$)

**RAGA** (XYLOPHONE or GLOCKENSPIEL)

*mp*

**DRONE** (KEYBOARD or BASS XYLOPHONE)

**INDIAN BELLS**

*mp*

v.1 In the tem - ple sit I, Watch - ing the birds who fly by.
v.2 Rain - bow col - ours I see, Flow - ers are look - ing at me.
v.3 I will paint all I see, Hop - ing to glor - i - fy thee.

**SHEET 1**

A WORLD OF LIGHT · SCHOFIELD & SIMS LTD   86

# Kori's Song

In and out And round a - bout, In the tem - ple sit I.
Smell - ing sweet A - round my feet. Rain - bow col-ours I see.
All a - round In beau - ty bound. I will paint all I see.

**CHORUS**

*mf*

God - dess Ka - li, I must be Like the birds, so set me free.
God - dess Ka - li, I must be Like the flow - ers, bright and free.
God - dess Ka - li, I must be Nat - ure's friend, so set me free.

87 A WORLD OF LIGHT · SCHOFIELD & SIMS LTD                SHEET 2

# Kori's Song

Use my col - ours, use my mind, Use my tal - ent for man - kind.
Use my col - ours, use my mind, Use my tal - ent for man - kind.
Use my col - ours, use my mind, Use my tal - ent for man - kind.

SHEET 3

**A WORLD OF LIGHT** · SCHOFIELD & SIMS LTD   88

# Kori's Song

**UNIT 9**
**A song for assembly based on the Hindu faith**

1. *(mp)* In the temple sit I,
   Watching the birds who fly by.
   In and out
   And round about,
   In the temple sit I.

   CHORUS I
   *(mf)* Goddess Kali, I must be
   Like the birds, so set me free.
   Use my colours, use my mind,
   Use my talent for mankind.

2. *(mp)* Rainbow colours I see,
   Flowers are looking at me.
   Smelling sweet
   Around my feet.
   Rainbow colours I see.

   CHORUS II
   *(mf)* Goddess Kali, I must be
   Like the flowers, bright and free.
   Use my colours, use my mind,
   Use my talent for mankind.

3. *(mf)* I will paint all I see,
   Hoping to glorify thee.
   All around
   In beauty bound.
   I will paint all I see.

   CHORUS III
   *(mf)* Goddess Kali, I must be
   Nature's friend, so set me free.
   Use my colours, use my mind,
   Use my talent for mankind.

## UNIT 10
### A story for assembly based on the Christian faith

# A Very Special Donkey

Two thousand years ago, on the Sunday before he was crucified, Jesus rode into the city of Jerusalem on a donkey and was welcomed by cheering crowds. People plucked palm branches from the palm trees and waved them shouting "Hosanna!" which means "God bless the king who comes in the name of the Lord." A few days later, on the day we know as Good Friday, Jesus who had entered Jerusalem as a king was crucified (nailed to a cross like a criminal). Three days later, the day we celebrate as Easter Sunday, anxious friends found the tomb where he had been buried was empty. The large boulder Pontius Pilate had ordered to be placed before the entrance had been rolled away. In the next few weeks, Jesus was to visit his friends and talk and even eat with them. He had died on the cross but he was alive and all his friends knew it and were able to say to others, "Our Lord really was the son of God."

And what happened to the donkey who carried Jesus so proudly into Jerusalem that day? Did he go back to his own stable and tell his animal friends, "I carried a king today?" Does the cross on the backs of so many donkeys tell us about a very special donkey who played such an important part in the first of the Sundays we call "Palm Sunday?"

The story this morning is about another very special donkey, one who led his friend to safety during a pit disaster in the Yorkshire town of Doncaster more than a hundred years ago.

In the eighteen-hundreds, children of your age and younger would often work for a living and one of the very worst jobs children had to do was to work down a coal mine or pit. Many mines had pit ponies or donkeys to pull the cartloads of coal, but often children were expected to do this job too. They would be chained to the carts and have to move forward on all fours, dragging the laden carts along the floor of the mine. The only lights would be from the wavering flames of candles stuck into helmets and if these should go out, the children would work in total darkness for hours, a frightening experience for anyone.

Joseph was the youngest of five children and he lived in Doncaster. His father and two older brothers worked down the mine and although Joseph was only seven years old, he too had to become a miner and work long hours – so long that sometimes his father had to carry his little son home because Joseph was too tired to walk.

Most of the younger children were too tired to talk to each other even if they met during the long hours they spent underground. Joseph had one friend in the mine, a blind pit donkey whom the little boy would call "Tufty". He would pat and stroke him whenever he had the chance. He wanted to bring the donkey home but his parents could not allow that. They could hardly afford to feed themselves as it was.

"Do you think we could send you, a little lad, to work all those hours down the pit if we didn't need the money?" asked his mother. She knew that Joseph shared his food with the donkey, and she gave him something extra when she could.

On Sundays the mines were closed and everyone was expected to go to church, children being sent to Sunday school in the afternoon. Joseph sang in the children's choir when he wasn't too tired. He was to sing the whole verse of an Easter hymn by

SHEET 1

A WORLD OF LIGHT · SCHOFIELD & SIMS LTD    90

# A Very Special Donkey

himself on Easter Sunday and his family would be there to listen to him.

It was the day before Palm Sunday that the disaster everyone would remember for the rest of their lives occurred. Everything was as usual when Joseph left his father and brothers to ride in the cage down to the floor of the mine. He patted the donkey as usual and the little animal nuzzled his hand. Later, Joseph would find a way of giving his four-legged friend a whole apple that his mother had given him, but there were many hours to get through before then and the foreman had told him he was to go deeper into one of the tunnels today to help one of the men.

"He's only seven," protested his father and the foreman nodded.

"I know but he's the quickest lad we've got among the little 'uns. He's a fast mover and if he does all right at filling up the cart I'll let him lead that stupid donkey he likes so much after work today."

Joseph heard this and he worked as hard as he could to fill the carts which the even younger boys were dragging through the darkness.

The roaring sound seemed far away at first but Jack, the man whom Joseph was helping, suddenly stopped chipping away at the tunnel wall.

"Did you hear that, Joe?" he asked. "Something's wrong."

Before Joseph could answer, there was a loud booming sound and then a bang which sent the boy hurtling to the ground. His candle went out and there was complete darkness.

"Jack!" shouted Joseph rushing towards where he last saw the man. "Are you all right?"

Jack seemed to be stretched out on the ground and by now the moans and cries could be heard. Joseph tried to move forward and fell over the bodies of two of the children he had just seen dragging carts along the narrow passageway. Joseph went on very carefully until he reached a wall and leaned against it. Someone was tapping and shouting on the other side and he tapped back again and shouted but there was no answer and in the end he turned away and sat down on the edge of an overturned cart and began to cry. No one would find him there. He was lost forever at the bottom of the mine and somewhere his father and his brothers were lost, too. He wanted his mother very badly but he would never see her again.

Joseph thought he saw something glowing in the darkness and he covered his face in fright. The glow came nearer. There was a gentle nudge on his arm and something licked his face. He was too frightened to make a sound and then he knew it was the donkey. He threw his arms around the animal's neck and cried again but the donkey kept on pushing him gently as if he were trying to tell Joseph something. Joseph struggled to his feet.

"He wants me to follow him," he thought, "but it's too dark. I'll lose him."

He had forgotten about the glow he had seen before the donkey actually reached him. As he stood the boy saw a light on the donkey's back. It was in the shape of a cross and Joseph could see very easily as he followed his friend.

Joseph seemed to be walking, stumbling, picking himself up and going on again for hours. They seemed to be going deeper and deeper into the earth but Joseph could see the glowing cross very easily and he trusted the donkey to find a way out even though, at times, he could hardly breathe for the coal dust and sometimes he fell and the donkey had to wait for him. At last, though it seemed a very long way away, Joseph saw a light in the distance. It grew bigger and bigger until Joseph knew they were out. How and where he did not know until he saw the sky above him and then he saw they were in the old disused quarry about a mile away from the mine.

Now it was his turn to lead the donkey for his friend was blind. He had played in the old quarry with his brothers many times and,

# A Very Special Donkey

though he was so tired he could hardly walk, he led the donkey slowly up through the slate and stones until, at last, they stood on firm ground.

After a short rest he tried to lead the donkey forward and even though he held on to the little tuft of hair on the animal's forehead and coaxed him gently, still the donkey did not move.

"Perhaps you want me to ride on your back, Tufty," said Joseph doubtfully and he struggled to mount the donkey who, once Joseph was safely on his back, began to move slowly forward.

The anxious, despairing crowd at the mine entrance had been there all night watching the rescue of the men and children. Mothers, wives and daughters watched and by midday of this Palm Sunday only a small number, mostly children, had still to be brought out.

"It might have been a lot worse," people were saying and Joseph's mother knew she was lucky in that her husband and older sons were safe if injured and yet she could not move from the mine, not until they brought Joseph out.

They could not go down again because it was feared there would be another explosion and the foreman had to tell Joseph's mother that he had sent Joseph into one of the tunnels and there was no way out.

Then there was a shout which changed to a cheer as two blackened figures came slowly into view. Joseph was in his mother's arms in seconds and as she hugged him she said firmly, "You'll never go down that pit again. Never."

"What about Dad and our Tom and Arthur?" asked Joseph as a doctor came forward to examine him.

"Safe," replied his mother. "Our Tom tried to go back for you and he hurt his leg but he'll soon be all right. They've all been taken to the school house to be seen by the doctors."

When the doctor had found that Joseph was unhurt he told the boy's mother to take him home.

"What about him, Mum?" Joseph pointed to the donkey. "He saved me. He can't be sent back."

"He's coming with us," answered his mother. "We'll manage somehow."

She went with Joseph to the donkey who was standing forlornly a few yards away.

"Come on, Tufty," Joseph said putting his arm around the donkey. "You've got a name and a home now."

The story has an even happier ending. The story of the rescue was printed in the newspapers and many people sent money for the donkey's keep. Although some of this was shared with the families who had lost someone in the disaster, so much arrived that Joseph's father was able to buy a small farm so that none of his family would ever need to go down the mine again. Tufty, the brave little donkey, became well and strong and although he was always blind he was happy and lived for many years. For the rest of his life, Joseph told the story of the cross on the donkey's back which had shone in the darkness and led a frightened little boy to safety.

# Donkey Song

**UNIT 10**
**A song for assembly based on the Christian faith**

**Lively** (♩ = 116)

*v.1* I'm a
spec - ial lit - tle donk - ey, I'm to take Je - sus to Jer - u - sa - lem. I am
spec - ial for He chose me, I'm to take Je - sus to Jer - u - sa - lem.

93  A WORLD OF LIGHT · SCHOFIELD & SIMS LTD

SHEET 1

# Donkey Song

On my first jour - ney, He is to ride me, Show me the way, My guide._____ v.2 I'm a hap - py lit - tle donk - ey, I'm tak - ing Je - sus to Jer - u - sa - lem.
hap - py for He loves me, I'm tak - ing Je - sus to Jer - u - sa - lem.

SHEET 2

A WORLD OF LIGHT · SCHOFIELD & SIMS LTD  94

1
2
mp (cresc.)
I am
Pat-ting me gent - ly, Waves to the crowd, Their
17
mp (cresc.)
CHORUS
TAMBOURINE
mf
f
arms reach for Him, They shout:
Sing! Sing! Sing!
21
mf
f

# Donkey Song

SHEET 4

# Donkey Song

Sing! Sing! Sing! Praise

I'm tak-ing Je - sus to Jer - u - sa-lem. I am hap-py for He loves me,

be to Him! Praise Him!

*(un poco rit)* *(a tempo)*

I'm tak-ing Je - sus to Jer - u - sa-lem. Praise Him!

**UNIT 10**

*A song for assembly based on the Christian faith*

# Donkey Song

1. *(mf)* I'm a special little donkey,
   I'm to take Jesus to Jerusalem.
   I am special for He chose me,
   I'm to take Jesus to Jerusalem.
   On my first journey,
   He is to ride me,
   Show me the way,
   My guide.

2. *(mf)* I'm a happy little donkey,
   I'm taking Jesus to Jerusalem.
   I am happy for He loves me,
   I'm taking Jesus to Jerusalem.
   *(mp cresc.)* Patting me gently,
   Waves to the crowd,
   Their arms reach for Him,
   *(mf)* They shout:

CHORUS
*(f)* Sing! Sing! Sing! Sing!
Praise be to Him!
Sing! Sing! Sing! Sing!
Praise be to Him!

I'm a special little donkey,
I'm taking Jesus to Jerusalem.
I am happy for He loves me,
I'm taking Jesus to Jerusalem.
Praise Him!

DESCANT
Sing!
Sing! Sing! Sing!
Praise be to Him!
Praise Him!

SHEET 1

A WORLD OF LIGHT · SCHOFIELD & SIMS LTD    98

# Samuel, the Boy Prophet

**UNIT 11**
**A play for assembly based on the Jewish faith**

**CHARACTERS**
Hannah, mother of Samuel
Samuel, a young boy of about eight years
Eli, an elderly priest
Israelite Elder
Voice of God

## Scene One

*Takes place in the ancient city of Shiloh. Inside the tent which serves as a temple, an old priest is sitting, deep in thought. Suddenly, a young woman enters, her face veiled. She thinks the temple is empty, takes off her veil and begins to weep. She controls herself, and prays aloud.*

**HANNAH**

Lord, if you will give me a son, I will give him back to you, so that he can serve you all his life.

*She begins to cry again.*

**ELI** *approaching her*

What are you doing here in this state? How dare you come drunk to the Temple? Take my advice. Go home, where you belong and stop this habit of taking too much wine.

**HANNAH**

I'm...I'm...not drunk...

**ELI** *sternly*

Of course you are. No self-respecting woman would walk alone through the streets and sit crying and talking to herself in the temple. It is disgusting. Who are you and where is your husband?

**HANNAH** *sadly*

My husband's name is Elkanah and he is with his other wife at present.

**ELI** *more kindly*

Is your husband unkind to you? Does he leave you alone too much that you have taken to drink?

**HANNAH** *firmly*

No, no. He is a wonderful husband and I haven't been drinking. I was praying to the Lord to take away my sadness and in return, I will do something for him.

**ELI** *sympathetically*

I see. I am sorry I thought you were drunk. You must have been desperate to come here

99  A WORLD OF LIGHT · SCHOFIELD & SIMS LTD

SHEET 1

# Samuel, the Boy Prophet

alone. Go in peace, my daughter. Then the Lord will grant you your request.

**HANNAH**

I hope that we will meet again and that next time you will have a better opinion of me.

*She rises to her feet and Eli places a hand on her head for a moment before she leaves.*

**ELI** *going to the door of the temple and watching her departure*

I have misjudged her. She is a good woman. May the Lord grant whatever it is she wants so desperately.

**ELDER** *entering*

Good afternoon, Eli. Was that Elkanah's wife I saw hurrying out of here a moment ago?

**ELI** *convinced*

Yes, it was. Do you know her?

**ELDER**

She comes here every year with Elkanah and his second wife and family. Hannah is a good woman, and Elkanah thinks highly of her, even though she has borne him no children.

**ELI**

Oh, so that was it. She was praying and crying and at first I thought her drunk and was stern with her.

**ELDER**

Poor Hannah. She was probably praying for a child. I doubt very much that Elkanah ever reproaches her but she must feel sad all the same when her husband's other wife has given him several children.

**ELI**

Children can be a great source of trouble sometimes. I should know.

**ELDER**

Yes, Eli, you should know, and as a priest with sons who are not fit to follow in your footsteps, you should do something about it.

**ELI** *hopelessly*

I have tried, but they won't listen to me.

**ELDER**

It is the way you have brought them up, Eli. You are a good man, but I should tell you that the people are bitter towards you. However, the Lord is your judge, not I. To return to Hannah...

*He continues to talk to Eli as the scene ends.*

SHEET 2

# Samuel, the Boy Prophet

## Scene Two

*Several years later, at the temple of Shiloh again. Hannah, much more happy and confident than she was on her last visit, enters the temple, holding a small boy by the hand.*

**ELI** *approaching*

Haven't I seen you somewhere before? I seem to remember...

**HANNAH** *quietly*

Several years ago I came here and prayed for a son. You thought I was drunk. I made a promise to the Lord that day, that if a son should be born to me, I would give him back to the Lord to be in his service. I am now fulfilling this promise. This is my son Samuel and I wish to place him in your care.

**ELI** *delighted*

May the Lord bless you with many more sons. Samuel, do you wish to live and work with me here in the temple?

**SAMUEL**

Yes, sir, I do.

**ELI**

Does he know you will be leaving him here?

**HANNAH**

Samuel knows.

*She bends down to speak to the boy.*

Samuel, your father and I will visit you every year and I will make new clothes for you each time. When you are older, of course, you will be able to visit us sometimes, but from now on you will live here. You know that, don't you?

**SAMUEL**

Yes, mother.

**ELI**

I will care for him and he will learn to look after the temple. Say goodbye to your mother, child. Your home will be with me now.

*Samuel kisses his mother, who hurries quickly away, the boy watching her go.*

**ELI** *cheerfully*

Well, Samuel, you and I are going to be great friends. I will show you where you will sleep, and then I'll teach you how to trim the temple lamps. Come with me now.

*The lights fade as Eli takes the child's hand to lead him out.*

A WORLD OF LIGHT · SCHOFIELD & SIMS LTD

SHEET 3

# Samuel, the Boy Prophet

## Scene Three

*An hour later. Samuel is lying on a mat in an alcove in a bare room.*

**ELI** *appearing right*

Goodnight, Samuel. I am only across the room from you, so if you wake in the night, don't be frightened. I shall be here.

**SAMUEL** *sleepily*

Yes. Goodnight, Eli.

*The lights fade. Suddenly, a voice is heard.*

**VOICE**

Samuel. Samuel.

**SAMUEL** *jumping up*

Yes, here I am.

*He runs across the room, and the lights come on and he is seen to shake Eli, who is sleeping on the other side of the room.*

**ELI**

What is it, Samuel?

**SAMUEL**

You called me. What do you want me for, Eli?

**ELI** *puzzled*

I didn't call you, Samuel. I was asleep. Go back to bed.

**SAMUEL**

Oh, yes, Eli.

*He hurries back to his bed and lies down.*

**VOICE**

Samuel. Samuel.

**SAMUEL** *springing out of bed*

Yes, Eli? I'm here.

**ELI**

Samuel, go back to bed. You were dreaming.

**SAMUEL**

But, Eli —

**ELI**

Go on, now. We'll never be up in the morning if you go on like this.

**SAMUEL** *sadly*

Yes, Eli.

*He hurries back to bed and lies down.*

SHEET 4

# Samuel, the Boy Prophet

**VOICE** *louder*

SAMUEL! SAMUEL!

**SAMUEL** *jumping out of bed*

Eli, you *did* call me. Three times I've heard your voice. Please believe me. Eli, I did hear you calling me.

**ELI** *patiently*

It's all right, Samuel. I understand now. I didn't call you, but God did. Go back to bed and when you hear the voice again, say, "Speak, Lord, for your servant hears you." Then listen carefully and tell me all that God says to you.

**SAMUEL**

"Speak, Lord, for your servant hears you." I'll remember.

*He walks slowly back to his bed.*

**VOICE**

Samuel. Samuel.

**SAMUEL**

Speak, Lord, for your servant hears you.

**VOICE**

I have a message for Eli which I want you to give to him tomorrow. Listen carefully. Eli is the High Priest and his sons, too, are priests under him. Usually sons become high priests after their fathers, but in this case it won't be so. Eli's sons are wicked, and they are not fit to become priests at all. They will not be high priests after their father. The descendants of Eli will not be priests after him. Eli, too, has been wicked, because he has done nothing to prevent his sons from behaving in a manner which is upsetting the people, yet he knows how bad his sons are. You are chosen to succeed Eli as High Priest of Israel, Samuel. Eli will train you for the time when you will succeed him.

**SAMUEL** *wonderingly*

Me, Lord? I am to succeed Eli?

**VOICE**

Yes, Samuel. You will be God's prophet and you will one day advise all Israel.

*The voice fades and after a few moments, Samuel lies down again, and there is silence.*

SHEET 5

# Samuel, the Boy Prophet

## Scene Four

*The following morning in the same room as before. Eli is heard calling for Samuel who hides behind a temple pillar.*

**ELI**

Samuel, where are you? I want to talk to you. Don't be afraid. I know you have a message for me, and I won't be angry whatever it is. Come out, Samuel. I know you are in here.

**SAMUEL** *emerging slowly*

Yes, Eli, I'm here.

**ELI** *taking the boy's hand and drawing him to his side*

Samuel, you must tell me what the Lord said to you because it is a message for me, isn't it?

**SAMUEL**

Yes, Eli, but it isn't a very nice message.

**ELI**

No, well. I didn't expect it to be. Tell me, please.

**SAMUEL** *sadly*

The Lord said that your sons are wicked men and that because you haven't tried to stop them, you are wicked too. I don't think you are wicked, Eli. The Lord said it.

**ELI** *quietly*

What else did the Lord say?

**SAMUEL**

That . . . that your sons would not be high priests after you, Eli?

**ELI** *sadly*

It is no more than I expected. Was that all?

**SAMUEL** *turning away*

Don't ask me any more, Eli.

**ELI** *sternly*

But I have asked you, and if you do not tell me, you are disobeying the Lord's command. Did the Lord say who would be High Priest after me? Did he, Samuel?

**SAMUEL** *embarrassed*

He. . . He said it would be me, Eli.

**ELI**

Well, that doesn't surprise me. Samuel, my sons have been on my mind for a long time, but I spoilt them when they were young, and they won't listen to me now. The best way for me to make up for that is to train you to take over after me. Don't be sad, Samuel. You were sent to me for a purpose and you will be a great prophet and leader. Now we will begin right away and you can learn how to look after the temple first of all. Come on.

# Samuel, the Boy Prophet

You have a lot to learn, but I think you will be such a great prophet that you will be remembered for ever.

**SAMUEL** *earnestly*

And you, Eli. I won't let anyone say anything against you.

**ELI**

It is too late for that, Samuel. People have been saying things about me for years. I am responsible for my sons' wickedness because I did not train them well enough. Well, I shall try to make up for it with you.

*He turns to walk slowly out as the play ends. Samuel follows.*

## UNIT 11
### A song for assembly based on the Jewish faith

# Samuel

(♩ = 63)

v.1 Sam - uel, Sam - uel, one night in the tem - ple,
v.2 Sam - uel, Sam - uel, you're the cho - sen per - son,
v.3 Sam - uel, Sam - uel, you will be their lead - er,

Sam - uel hears a voice of heav'n - ly love. Speak - ing in the
Sam - uel, you have spe - cial work to do. Sent to help your
Sam - uel, you will show them all the way. Guid - ing them through

\* Recorder can play the melody if desired.

SHEET 1

A WORLD OF LIGHT · SCHOFIELD & SIMS LTD   106

# Samuel

still - ness, Speak - ing through the dark - ness, Sam - uel, list - en!
peo - ple, Sent to be their proph - et, Sam - uel, list - en!
dan - ger, Guid - ing them to safe - ty, Sam - uel, list - en!

*vv.1&2*
God calls from a - bove.
God is cal - ling you.

*v.3*
God is trust - ing you,_____ Kneel and pray.

### UNIT 11
### A song for assembly based on the Jewish faith

# Samuel

1. *(mp)* Samuel, Samuel, one night in the temple,
   Samuel hears a voice of heav'nly love.
   Speaking in the stillness,
   Speaking through the darkness,
   *(mf)* Samuel, listen! God calls from above.

2. *(mf)* Samuel, Samuel, you're the chosen person,
   Samuel, you have special work to do.
   Sent to help your people,
   Sent to be their prophet,
   Samuel, listen! God is calling you.

3. *(mf)* Samuel, Samuel, you will be their leader,
   Samuel, you will show them all the way.
   *(mp)* Guiding them through danger,
   *(cresc.)* Guiding them to safety,
   *(mf)* Samuel, listen! God is trusting you,
   *(p)* Kneel and pray.

SHEET 1

**HARRINGTON HILL PRIMARY SCHOOL**
HARRINGTON HILL
LONDON E5 9LH
TEL: 0181 806 7275  FAX: 0181 806 3364